OFFICER HONEY

LIGHT IN THE DARKNESS

OFFICER HONEY

LIGHT IN THE DARKNESS

HONEY FRENCH

Rock Publishing

Copyright © Honey French

Printed in the United States of America
Second Printing

Published by
Rock Publishing
P. O. Box 775
Grover Beach, CA 93483

Cover and text design by Marlon Villadiego

Unless otherwise noted, all scripture references are taken from the
Holy Bible, the King James Version (KJV).

ISBN -13: 978-0615593142 (Rock Publishing)
ISBN -10: 0615593143

For licensing / copyright information, for additional copies or for
use in specialized settings contact:

Honey French
www.HoneyFromTheRockMinistry.com
P. O. Box 775
Grover Beach, California 93483

DEDICATION

This book is dedicated to my dear friend Shawn Hardin.

I'm so grateful and appreciative of her unceasing prayers

for me to fulfill God's purpose for my life.

Son Steve Moy and Daughter Laurie Moy,

thank you for forgiving my past mistakes and loving me anyway.

My spiritual sons Paul and David,

thank you for your continuous prayers for me.

What a thrill to see the men of God you are.

To the courageous Correctional officers who risk their lives

working daily with dangerous, violent offenders.

TABLE OF CONTENTS

FOREWORD

"Officer Honey" is an interesting, entertaining, and sometimes challenging story, a book that reads quickly and grippingly. Its subject is an accurate portrayal of the Honey Moy French that we have grown to love and appreciate over the past several years.

Growing up isolated and a victim of prejudice, her story gives you insight to the struggles that many young people faced in small town America. Creatively working her way through adolescence she arrives at adulthood via a culture that empowers pleasure and self-indulgence. She makes some amazing discoveries that transforms her life from "being a taker to a giver."

The spiritual discoveries alter her destiny, and with a new heart and attitude of accomplishment, she makes her way as a forerunner into a career that is uncharted by women. In an atmosphere of oppression, deceit, and hopelessness, Honey becomes a source of new beginnings for the people around her.

My wife and I have known Honey for several years and know that these adventures are accurate and well known in our region of the Central Coast of California. Her personal faith is authentic, and with great courage in the face of potential repercussions, she demonstrates that faithfulness to the purposes of God results in miracles. She has prayed with hundreds of people as they have dedicated themselves to God and hundreds more to receive the baptism of the Holy Spirit and physical healings.

With a petite physique, the anointing on her life demands great respect from even the largest and most hardened criminals. The grace of an evangelist flows through her and regularly melts the hearts of those once hostile to God. Whether in the workplace, a supermarket, on the street, or in our church service, Honey is consistently looking for opportunities to witness and minister to the lost and broken. Her theology is practical, her revelation of Jesus is authentic, and I would recommend her to any ministry situation that may arise in the future.

Pastor and friend,

Patrick Sparrow
Senior Pastor
Shouts of Grace Church
ACTS Churches USA

INTRODUCTION

My purpose in writing this book is to honor God and to show God's heart of love for those who are hurt and damaged by life's circumstances. – Both those suffering through no fault of their own and also those whose wrong choices cause their pain.

I hope to encourage prison staff, families who have incarcerated love ones, prisoners, and those who are just having difficulty coping with life.

My story illustrates how my sorrows weren't wasted, but instead were eventually used for my good and the benefit of others. The stories demonstrate how God can use the unqualified to accomplish His purposes.

To open the blind eyes, to bring out the prisoners from the prison, and them that sit in darkness out of the prison house.
Isaiah 42:7

And I will bring the blind by a way that they knew not; I will lead them in paths that they have not known: I will make darkness light before them and crooked things straight. These things will I do unto them and not forsake them.
Isaiah 42:16

The steps of a good man are ordered by the LORD: and he delights in his way.
Psalm 37:23.

Trust in the LORD with all thine heart; and lean not unto thine own understanding. In all thy ways acknowledge him, and he shall direct thy paths.
Proverbs 3:5 and 6

CHAPTER 1

ALONE AND TERRIFIED

Clang! The heavy prison grille gate slammed shut behind me, locking me in. I tried in vain to hide the shudder causing a shiver to run through me. I wondered if I'd ever get used to the crashing sound the gate made as it closed. It felt so final, so claustrophobic, so cruel. I wondered if that's what it sounded like to inmates locked up behind the thick, drab-colored prison walls. Did each harsh sound of metal grating against metal bring a greater sense of hopelessness and despair?

I followed close behind the others, ignored the curious stares of the inmates I was passing, and focused straight ahead. I tried to appear confident. Oh how I hoped my uneasiness and apprehension wouldn't be apparent.

What was I doing in this dreadful place -- a prison? Well, I started working as one of the first women correctional officers in a prison housing male felons. -- All 5'2" and 104 pounds of me! How did I get there? What made me even *want* to be an officer? I *always* wanted to help people change for the better. My goal was to combine work experience with education to become a correctional counselor. I felt I was finally fulfilling a life-time wish. I didn't know then that dream would be delayed by harsh reality. What even gave me that desire? Let me describe my background.

As long as I could remember my mom and dad had yelling and screaming, sometimes violent arguments continually. When Dad's car came into the driveway, Mom would hiss, "The bastard's home." We would become tense with fear and apprehension. Dad was like a volcano...and as unpredictable. Would Dad be drunk, in a rage, or both? We never knew what to expect.

Most often Dad would come home from work, change his clothes, and leave. As a child, I didn't know why my daddy didn't want to stay home. That was one of many unanswered questions. I concluded that there must be something terribly wrong with *me* for him not to want to be with us. I felt rejected, ashamed, lonely, empty inside, and abandoned – like an old western movie set – desolate with the wind blowing through the half torn shutters.

Mom was beautiful and sophisticated. She was as sleek and elegant as her long, slim cigarette holders, which seemed to be always between her bejeweled fingers. She had several to match her various outfits. However in sharp contrast, when she was alone in the house with her three young daughters, vulgar cursing and profane name-calling were sprinkled throughout her tirades against Dad and his "whore."

She used to be the belle of every dance when she was young. Being much sought after in her youth must have made Dad's betrayal even more poignantly painful and humiliating.

I felt I had this big, terrible secret I couldn't share with anyone. I was the oldest, the next daughter was 5-1/2 years younger, and the third daughter was 1-1/2 years younger than her, so they were too young to talk to about such issues. We lived out in the country without neighbors my age. I wouldn't have a friend visit anyway, since I never knew what would happen next in our house. This constant fearful uncertainty and tension caused deep feelings of insecurity and loneliness.

And at school I didn't feel really accepted either, since I was the only minority in the whole school until the fourth grade. Classmates would be friends one moment, but then the next instant when they were bored, I had to tolerate the racial insults, jeers, and ridicule hurled at me: Chink! Chinaman! Slant Eyes!

I wouldn't let myself cry, but I couldn't keep my eyes from tearing up at times. Since hurt and shame were my constant companions, I was always on guard, fearing more rejection.

And yet desperately longing for acceptance, I would try to be friendly. And when we had our first male teacher, he terrified me because he was so tall and appeared to be so stern. And when he caught me talking to someone during class, which was frequent, his voice would boom out loudly calling my name. Finally he tired of trying to curb my verboseness and ordered me to drag my desk to the front of the class next to his desk and turn it around. It was horrible to have to be in front, facing the class while they snickered. A couple times of forced public isolation cured my chattiness.

One memory is indelibly imprinted into my mind. While sitting in our fifth grade class at the beginning of the period, Bob, who I considered friendly, suddenly and unexpectedly starting singing,

"Ching chong chinaman sitting on a rail…"

My face flushed and felt burning hot. My stomach knotted up with that old, familiar, sick feeling. I felt so embarrassed I just wanted to disappear. I wanted to pretend his words didn't penetrate and hurt. I ignored the gaping wound in my heart and finished the song with him,

"Along came a train cutting off his tail."

Instantly, I felt bathed in shame for reciting that verse. I had betrayed my own ancestry.

Suddenly our teacher appeared beside my desk. His deep voice thundered at Bob, "Don't...you...EVER... make fun of ANY of my students again!" Bob shrank back in his seat. I was still very embarrassed; but from that day on, I considered the once-feared-by-me Mr. Duncan to be my knight in shining armor. He rescued me from that horrible, mortifying predicament. It was years later that I realized the tail probably meant the long braided hair that went down the railroad workers' backs. But then I thought it meant my tormentors considered Chinese to be like monkeys.

Recess wasn't any fun either. I was always one of the left-over, inept losers a team was forced to take. During baseball season I was put where they thought I would do the least damage: way far out in centerfield. But when, horror of horrors, a ball would occasionally get to me, my throwing arm was so weak I had a hard time getting it to the infield. I would heave it with all my might, run the few feet it went, pick it up, and heave it again. Sometimes I would repeat the process three throws. It didn't occur to me it would have been just as fast to just hold the ball and run it to the infield. It's funny now when I remember back, but then it was terribly embarrassing. Adding to my humiliation, others on my team shook their heads in disgust and blamed me as the opposing team's runners crossed home plate.

At home things weren't getting any better. Every now and then, probably when I was around eight, Mom would take me to park in front of the "whore's" house in the middle of the night. She insisted I accompany her because she didn't want to be in the dark alone. I hated it when we went. It was cold and scary sitting for hours in the darkness of that car. Mom would mutter profanities and threats about what she would do if she found Dad and that woman together. I was terrified of what would happen if that did occur. I wanted to be in my warm bed instead of in that cold car listening to Mom rant and rave. But I knew better than to protest or complain.

To add to my insecurity, I was terribly nearsighted. But I didn't tell anyone I couldn't see the blackboard at school because Mom would remark quite often, "Poor so and so. Boys never make passes at girls that wear glasses." And I liked boys and wanted them to like me.

Every time the teacher wrote out a math problem, a sentence to diagram for English class, or a homework assignment on the blackboard, I'd get that sick feeling of dread again. I'd whisper to someone in one of the desks near me to try to find out what was written. Finally in the fourth grade, my teacher caught me whispering. When I admitted I couldn't see, she sent me to the school nurse, who wrote a note instructing my mom to get my eyes examined by an optometrist.

My eyeglasses opened up the world to me in a wondrous way. I could see individual street lamps at night instead of a large, fuzzy blob of light. I remember sitting on the couch in the living room marveling at how I could actually see distinct, separate books instead of just a vague blur of colors.

The thick lens of my glasses caused my nearsighted eyes to appear smaller. I had round, owlish-looking, flesh-colored frames because they were the cheapest. Mom walked into the room. She shook her head disapprovingly. "Poor Honey." I knew she meant that now boys would find me even less attractive. The vogue of the day was colored cat-eyed-shaped frames.

I put my eyeglasses away into the case and only took them out to see the blackboard. The rest of the time I went around not seeing well enough to know who was across the street, or whether the person sitting across the room was looking at me or someone else, and whether that person was smiling or frowning. Vanity had a strong grip on me at an early age.

Once at a new restaurant, I was searching for the restroom. Someone came toward me and we did that little side-to-side dance trying to pass each other. I marveled how similar her dress was to mine. As I got closer I was mortified to discover the mirror on the door. I had been dancing with myself! Shame faced, I quickly looked around. Did anyone notice the spectacle I made of myself? Whew, no one had noticed! Relieved, I chuckled to myself.

The graduation celebration from our elementary school was to be held at a park with a pool. I had heard they didn't let minorities swim in the pool. I was really scared and for weeks dreaded the fast-approaching date. I feared it would turn into another humiliating experience. Thankfully though, there wasn't such a ruling, and my fears were unwarranted; but how I had suffered in the interim.

The rejection I experienced in school paved the way for more future rejection.

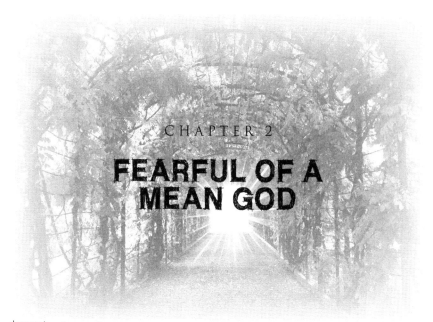

CHAPTER 2

FEARFUL OF A MEAN GOD

Earlier when I was around nine or ten, a friend invited me to church. Mom didn't investigate what their beliefs were. I can understand how it would be nice for her to have my two sisters and me out of the house on Sundays. It was a very strict church. They didn't believe in women wearing lipstick or pants or anyone going to movies.

And occasionally when Mom did drop my sisters and me off at the movies, I felt *so* horrible standing in front of a theater waiting for Mom to pick us up afterward. I wanted to hide. What if someone from that church drove by and saw me in front of that wicked, sinful place? It didn't matter if it was a wholesome Bambi or Lassie movie. I really had confused, mixed-up emotions. I wanted to see the movies and enjoyed them, but I felt so terribly guilty and evil afterward.

That church talked a lot about hell but not about the love of God. One night I was in bed and saw and felt myself falling, falling in stygian blackness for eternity! I don't know if I was awake or had dreamed it. I didn't want to go to hell! Terrified, I got up and

Chapter 2

prayed, confessed I was a sinner, and asked God into my heart. But I didn't feel any better. I felt so let down. Here it was so terribly hard to make that decision, and when I finally did, it appeared nothing happened.

The next day I asked the only Christian girl I knew if she "felt anything" when she "got saved". She told me she felt good. After suffering a childhood of rejection, I thought, "I guess I didn't do it right. Or I'm not good enough. Anyway, for whatever reason, God didn't accept me. God rejected me, too."

People in that church would go up to me, stick their finger in my face, and ask if I was "saved". I would mumble something and walk away. I didn't know for certain, but figured I must not be. I stopped attending church after awhile.

When I was a little older, I would watch a Billy Graham Crusade on television with mixed emotions. Part of me was hoping God would accept me and change me, and another part of me was fearful and dreading that He might. Then when the program was over, I had ambivalent feelings of disappointment interlaced with relief...disappointment that God didn't want me but relief that nothing happened. You see, to me at that time giving your life to God meant a dreadful future, like going to Africa to be a missionary. Since Dad was the authority figure in my life, God must be mean like him, I subconsciously reasoned.

I had confused, mixed-up feelings about God. One Sunday school teacher, at another church I attended for a short while, had given me a book about a transient young man who was changed dramatically by God. It thrilled me and I wondered, "Can I dare believe that God would have a good life for me if I surrendered?"

And I enjoyed reading a weekly column that had poems and stories about a vague God. In my young heart, I had a fleeting desire to write for God one day. But I dismissed that likelihood as being too impossible for someone as warped as I.

8

During my junior high years, while the other girls wore sweaters, skirts, fluffy angora sox, and oxfords, I wore my older cousin's discarded women's dresses and sandals. And I still had the horrible-looking, perfectly round, flesh-tinted eyeglasses instead of the style of the day, colored eyeglass frames in different designs. Outwardly I looked like the "square" outcast I felt inwardly that I was.

I purposely developed the habit of not being observant. I wouldn't pay attention to directions while riding in a car. I somehow had the muddled reasoning that if I didn't know the way home, I wouldn't be responsible for not seeing street signs without the glasses I refused to wear.

I'm not sure how old I was the night my father almost killed my mother...

SHAPED BY REJECTION

But before I describe that traumatic experience, I want to explain how my self-esteem was further damaged unknowingly by my parents. I was never hugged or kissed by them. They were so filled with their own problems, it overwhelmed and blinded them to the needs of their three daughters.

I felt very terribly alone and isolated my whole adolescent life. I had no friends because our home was "out in the country" with no one my age living near. I had no one, absolutely no one. There was no comforting adult to confide in ever. I was never held or kissed or told I was loved. My one grandparent was unapproachable.

I retreated into the world of books...mostly dog and horse stories...then Heidi, Pollyanna, and all the books in the Nancy Drew series were my companions. Books were my friends, and I found refuge in this world of fantasy in the midst of continuous strife, fear, tension, and turmoil. I escaped into books as often as I could.

When I was probably around eight, the daughter of my mom's friend was dropped off to visit. I was apprehensive as I never "played" with anyone before. My alarm turned to near panic. What do you do? I had no idea...not an inkling. Somehow we had a pretty good time despite my anxiety. Since she lived far away, we didn't see each other often, though.

In addition to reading, I had another passion. My home town accommodated the minor league baseball team The Sacramento Solons. Because Mom said Dad wanted a son, I applied myself to memorizing the wins and losses of the team's top pitchers and the batting averages of the best hitters.

One of my greatest thrills was to go watch the Solons with Dad. Even though we hardly talked at all, it was still fun for me. I didn't care if the hot dog bun was cold and hard, it still tasted good. I enjoyed the smells and the sounds, especially the crack of the bat hitting a ball and the dull thud of the ball going into the catcher's mitt, the excitement and roar of the crowd when someone on our team stole a base, the suspense.

But Mom said when I returned, "He didn't really want to go with you, you know. He asked all his friends first. No one could go. You were last choice." The momentary feeling of love and acceptance I felt vanished.

Our birthday gifts came signed "Love, Mom and Dad." But Mom always would tell us, "I signed it as being from both of us, but he doesn't even know it's your birthday. He's not here, is he?"

Years later when I was a young mother, one memorable day, Dad phoned! All he said was, "I just wanted to wish you a Happy Birthday." With that said, he hung up immediately. I sat there and sobbed for two hours. My dad *remembered* my birthday!

Now back to that horrendous night...

CHAPTER 4

NIGHT OF TERROR

They were having another huge argument and were yelling and screaming at each other. They often argued violently, but this time it was worse. I remember the terror...my heart pounding wildly...its rapid beating thundered in my ears...my two sisters and I remained in our rooms petrified...The two were upstairs, and my room was downstairs. We heard thuds, sounds of things banging around. Then we heard my mom's voice turn fearful and muffled as she screamed and sobbed, "Stop it! Stop choking me, Harry! You're hurting me!"

I was the oldest of the three daughters but Brenda, the next oldest, was the bravest at that moment.

She yelled, sobbing, "Leave her alone! Leave her alone! Get away from her! Stop hurting her! Stop hurting her!"

We could tell by the sounds that Mom broke away. We heard her sobbing and then shakily say she was calling the police. She was having a difficult time trying to find the number of the police through her tears.

CHAPTER 4

"I should help her find the phone number," I thought. But I feared my father's wrath. I just sat there woodenly on the edge of my bed. We heard her finally find the number and call for help and knew the police were on their way.

I sat numbly on my bed wondering if I would be questioned. I worried. What should I say if they questioned me? No matter what I said, one of them would be mad at me. Should I change from my nightgown or just put on a bathrobe. Or should I put on a blouse and pants? Should I put on lipstick?

Mom decided not to press charges. It would be too humiliating for her to have people know. I heard my dad talking to the policemen outside near my window trying to get them to condone his behavior. "You know how women are and how they can get to you...."

No one ever talked about what happened that night.

For years after that, I suffered guilt for even worrying about my appearance that night. What kind of an evil, vain person was I, worrying about how I looked when my parents' world was crumbling even further? It was years later before I would realize that dwelling on my appearance was a defense mechanism. I was trying to escape into something mundane and ordinary in order to survive that terrifying event. It felt safer to think of something familiar and commonplace, instead of the horror of that moment.

But there was another type of fear to experience...

PRIDE AND PREJUDICE

O n our very first day in gym class in junior high, we were told we were to team up in fours to share a shower area together. I got that familiar sick feeling in my stomach again from fear of rejection and humiliation. I feared no one would want me to be with them because I was Chinese. Thankfully that fear was unwarranted.

We had a teacher who emulated the movie actress Tallulah Bankhead and called everyone daaaahrling. You could smell her overpowering, intrusively offensive perfume moments before she dramatically swept into the room. I found a mistake on one of her tests, but she said I didn't understand the question because my English wasn't good enough. Curiously enough, it was Bob the boy who chanted Ching Chong Chinaman who came to my rescue. Bob spoke up and said, "She was born here. Her English is better than all of ours." If I hadn't totally forgiven him before, it was then a totally done deal.

Once while attending a war movie in a theater, my mom kept muttering out loud, "Those damn Japs!" I felt bad because some of my best friends were Japanese who attended our rival school. But even though I was embarrassed, I was inwardly glad she was saying that, so people sitting near us wouldn't think we *were* Japanese. Of course I felt guilty I was glad. I hated to hear any derogatory racial slurs against any race. I knew the sting of those wounding words and the indelible imprint they made on a soul, and I didn't want to hurt anyone the way I was hurt.

I caught the bus to and from work as a salesgirl after school on Fridays and eight hours on Saturday at a Dollar Store. The manager was very strict. If there were no customers, we had to mess up a table full of 5/$1 panties and stand there folding them into neat stacks again. We could never sit the whole eight hours.

I remember one of my most embarrassing experiences as a teenager there. It would be quite hot at the store with our smocks on during Sacramento's hot summers of 100+ degree weather and only fans in the store for cooling. So we women clerks would take our blouses off instead of wearing them under the smocks. The 80+ year-old male manager happened to come up the stairs and caught a glimpse of me in my slip reaching for the smock. Oh, I was mortified! I was a very modest 15 year-old teen. I was determined to quit the job rather than face the man again. But the other women reasoned with me and talked me into staying. But I still averted my gaze and couldn't look him in the face for weeks.

And before that, during the last year of junior high I learned to sew. As I made my own clothes, my appearance improved, and I gained more confidence.

"Our group" consisted of eight girls from two high schools. Every week we went to the movies, bowled, and/or stopped at Walgreens for chocolate cokes. Some of the girls could do all three, and some of us had to choose one or two of the activities depending on our finances. We giggled and shared secrets. It felt so good to "belong" at last.

And one in our group had an older brother who was in the

popular crowd. We wondered why those boys all had a long fingernail on their littlest finger. We gave her instructions to find out the meaning of this mystery. Oh were we disappointed and disgusted to learn their secret. The long fingernail was used to pick their noses!

The only time I received attention was when I got straight "A's", which I made sure to do consistently. Unfortunately that later carried over into adulthood. I had to be among the best in swim class, bowling league, dancing, and later as a housewife. What a strain that became. I couldn't relax and just have fun. If I couldn't be really good in an activity, I just wouldn't participate.

Boys suddenly discovered me during high school. I dated many boys but stayed a "good," moral girl. Enduring such a traumatic childhood, one would expect that I would have been immoral and promiscuous. That would come much later.

TEEN TRAUMA -- ?!

In the ninth grade I was eligible to join the Wah Lungs, a teen girls' club that gave monthly dances at the YWCA. I had mixed emotions each Thursday before the dance. It was almost like when I had a Friday dental appointment. I was glad it would be the weekend because I loved to sleep late instead of getting up early for school...Yet I almost dreaded the upcoming dance. Would boys ask me to dance or would I be a wall flower? I wasn't in the group of "the most popular girls."

And to complicate matters I wouldn't wear glasses to the dance. Because it was very dark, when several of us girls were standing together and a brave boy came up to ask one of us to dance, I couldn't see his eyes to tell which girl he was asking. A couple of times I learned afterward a boy had asked me first, and when I didn't respond, he asked the girl next to me. Oh how I didn't want to be labeled as being "stuck-up and too particular." Plus I would never knowingly hurt any boy's feelings by refusing him a dance.

Then some popular boys from a near-by town started attending and were attracted to me. They asked me to dance, and then three of them started dating me, and that made me popular with the other boys, too.

Also at 15 I had a crush on Dave. He was five years older than I. He hung around the men's store talking to me while I cashiered at my new job. I wondered why he stood with me while I waited to catch a bus home instead of offering me a ride. At the monthly dances our girls' club gave, he would hold me close and dance cheek to cheek but never asked if he could take me home. It never occurred to me he didn't own a car. I learned later he was saving his money for one. Dave was the first man that caused me to feel a "thrilling tingle" zing through me when we danced close together.

Then Dave went into the army and we corresponded. I was elated when he was home on leave and took me to the New Year's Eve Dance. I wore a sophisticated black dress and looked much older than 15. There I met Ron, a handsome college man. He was among the many who danced with me. After the dance Dave was stationed in Japan and then Korea and we continued exchanging letters.

Ron phoned me to ask me out soon after the NY Eve Dance. He was shocked and thought I was kidding when I said I would let him know after I asked my parents. He couldn't believe I could never go out without their permission. I debated what to wear the night he took me to a movie. I decided on a sweater and skirt and bobby sox. When I saw him I wished I had dressed up more. He looked handsome in his sports jacket.

It was drizzly out, and my hair immediately drooped. I tried to hide it with a bandana which kept slipping off my limp hair. So I kept fussing with it, trying unsuccessfully to keep my hair hidden under it. To make matters worse and adding to my discomfort, I also had a horrible cold and couldn't breathe during the whole movie. I didn't want to blow my nose and couldn't breathe through my nose without making disgusting sounds so had to breathe through my mouth. My lips soon became dry and chapped from breathing that way. I was utterly miserable.

After the movie he asked if I wanted to eat. I said "no" thinking he'd like me more if he didn't have to spend much money on me so just asked for a soda. He asked me again and then said, "Well, I'm eating!" His hamburger sure smelled delicious. I wished I had ordered one, too. How I wished he would offer me some, but he devoured it all.

His hunger satisfied, he asked, "Are you 19? No?.....22?.... 20?....21?....Then you must be 18? Surely you can't be 23?....17?..... Not 16?.....No, you CAN'T be 15?" He was absolutely horrified to learn I *was* only 15. Well, I guessed right: He never called again.

Later I dated a star basketball player Greg who was considered to be a real catch. I was thrilled when he asked me to a formal dance. I used to think there shouldn't be any lulls in conversations. Now I know they're a good thing many times, as people are reflecting on what was said or just savoring the moment of being together. We were with another couple in the lobby during intermission at the dance. There was an awkward lull. So I plunged in with a nervous, "Oh, what interesting wall paper." There was a stunned, uncomfortable silence. Of course I wasn't wearing my glasses. As we later walked back to the dance floor, and we got closer to that interesting wall paper, I discovered to my horror and embarrassment, it was wood parquet paneling!

One night after a date, I discovered Greg had sneaked a bottle of whiskey from the dining room table near our front door and carried it away as a prank. Dad had put it there to take fishing at 5 am the next day. Worry and fear delayed my longed-for escape into sleep.

Abruptly, I was wakened from my fitful sleep by Dad's loud cursing and yelling, "Where the hell is the f___ing damn bottle?!"

I pretended to be asleep. But my heart was wildly pounding so loudly I was terrified he would somehow hear it and know I was awake. Stress and fear caused me not to think rationally.

"So that's what they mean when they say their 'heart is in their throat' – ?"

He slammed the door, still cursing. I felt limp with relief as gratitude engulfed me. Thank God, he left! My fears didn't materialize.

When Greg brought the bottle back a day or so later, Mom berated him and emphasized over and over what a stupid act that was. I worried that he'd never dare ask me out again.

There was a big formal dance coming up. One by one over the eight weeks before the dance, five really nice boys asked me if they could be my escort. I had dated them before and liked each one, but I was hoping that Greg would ask me to be his date. It got closer and closer to the night of the dance. So at the monthly dance, I asked one of the boys who had previously asked me if he still wanted to take me. But he had already asked someone else. My face flamed red. I was already embarrassed to ask him and then doubly, horribly embarrassed by his answer. "Serves me right," I thought to myself.

Then a few days later while in a car with a group, Nick, a fellow I recently met, asked me if I wanted to go to the dance with him. It suddenly got quiet in the car, and I whispered I'd tell him later. I didn't know what to do, because Jim was in the front seat of the car with us, and he was one of the ones who had asked me earlier. I wanted to say yes to Nick, but I had already told Jim and the others I had a date.

By this time I felt desperate, realizing Greg, the one I was waiting for, wasn't going to ask me. To add to my dilemma, I was an officer in the group sponsoring the dance. If I didn't go and wasn't in the group photo of officers, everyone in the future and forever (!) would think I couldn't get a date, when in reality, six boys had asked me. So when Nick phoned later, I said yes making up a lie that the fellow who asked me first couldn't go for some reason.

And then about two weeks before the dance, while on a date with Nick, we were "necking" and he asked if I would elope with him immediately that night. He said another girl wanted him to marry her. He showed me a picture of her. She was really pretty and looked sexy with one shoulder bared in the photo. But she was wild, and I was a nice, sweet girl, he explained, the kind you marry.

He was a good kisser, and for a moment I crazily thought it would be nice to get out of the stress in our house. But then I remembered I had plain-looking underwear on, and I didn't want him to see it. Thank God for that plain bra and panty!

It turned out Nick never did take me to that dance. He had gotten that sexy girl pregnant, and her dad was forcing him to marry her. That's why he wanted to elope with me. It was so he wouldn't have to marry her. I was so selfish, I was more concerned about not having a date for the dance than the fact he and that poor pregnant girl had to marry when they weren't really in love.

I ended up phoning my good-looking cousin and begging him to take me to the dance. He showed up with two friends. At the dance he soon left me with one of them while he took off with the other guy. I didn't think the one who stayed was up to my dating standards. I was horribly mortified. When I finally got home, I cried and cried and cried. I truly thought I would never ever be able to overcome the humiliation of that dreadful night of agony and embarrassment. How could I show my face in public again? What made it worse was the knowledge that it was what I deserved after weaving that web of deception.

Well I did recover. Soon I had another crush on a cute, young boy two years older than I. He looked like a Chinese version of a young Albert Finney. We dated quite awhile; but when he went into the army, he wanted me to go steady and wait for him and not date the three months he would be away. Three whole long months?! How could I? That was a whole summer vacation. At that time, being 16, three whole long months seemed like an eternity to me!

The letters continued to fly between Dave and me. And even after I described in a letter my humiliating experience at that dreadful dance, he was still falling in love with me ...

HOW DID I GET ENGAGED -- ?!

Dave returned from his army service overseas just in time to be my date graduation night. He was 5-1/2 years older than I and seemed so manly and mature compared to the boys I had been dating. There was only one problem. My mom approved of him. She liked him so much she kept telling me how polite and nice he was. That made me wonder what was wrong with him. She had never liked anyone I was attracted to before. So I suspiciously looked for flaws in Dave.

Despite my puzzlement over Mom's encouragement, Dave and I dated steadily, and my feelings for him deepened into love.

I started working as a stenographer for the Dept. of Corrections Administration utilizing my shorthand skills. I didn't realize at the time that God was guiding my path before I really knew Him personally. At work I read some tragic case histories of men who were incarcerated. And one of the bosses gave me the book Prisoners Are People. Corrections also had an annual dinner and tour of a State prison. I was so impressed, most of the prisoners looked young and clean cut, not like the criminals in movies.

All of this was instilling within me empathy and compassion for prisoners.

Dave and I were still dating a lot, and our dates consisted of movies or bowling and having vegetable beef soup afterward. We both liked it, so he bought a case of it, since soup was a good alternative to the drive-in hamburgers he couldn't afford. He was saving money for our future.

We did a lot of heavy kissing and petting steaming up the interior of the car, and he had asked me to go steady three times. The fourth time he asked, I heard a voice inside telling me to say Yes. I thought that must be God since I didn't want to. So I said Yes. Immediately I experienced a sinking feeling of dread and regret. But Dave was so happy, I couldn't take it back, and especially since I thought it was God telling me to.

Not long afterward Dave and I were walking in downtown Sacramento. I remember how startled I was to see *her*! In front of me was The Other Woman who Mom called The Whore.

As soon as I recognized her, a rage suddenly overtook me. *She* was why Dad was hardly ever home... *She* was why I felt abandoned and rejected... *She* was why I wore my older cousin's discarded women's dresses and sandals while other teens at school wore sweaters, skirts, bobby sox, and oxfords... *She* was why I wore owlish eyeglasses instead of more expensive stylish ones.... *She* was why I felt like such a loser. *She* was why Dad never attended any of my birthdays or school events... *She* was why my daddy never loved me... *She* was the reason we lived this terrible, shameful, secret life. This reasoning wasn't entirely accurate, but at the time those thoughts consumed me.

Fraught with rage, I followed close behind her. I shouted loudly, "You whore...you bitch...you slut...you home wrecker," as she fled down the sidewalk. All those names my mother had uttered for so many years poured out of me in a torrent of accusations. I screamed these words over and over as she tried to get away from me. I didn't care that people were staring curiously. I wanted to hurt her the way she had hurt me! Finally she crossed the busy street as the light turned red and escaped my fury.

I was in a daze as Dave helped me to his car. I had forgotten all about him. He had followed a little behind me not knowing what else to do. I sat shaking and sobbing, uncontrollably, for about two hours. Finally, feeling exhausted and drained emotionally, I returned home.

I found Mom in the kitchen and described the recent scene in a tumble of words and tears. I expected comfort and vindication. After all, I felt I had stood up for her and my two sisters and me. I was absolutely shocked when Mom turned on me angrily.

"What's the matter with you? Now your dad will be hell to live with. What a stupid thing to do!"

Stunned, I turned and ran to my room. I threw myself on the bed crying. I pounded my fists into the bed. "I hate her, I hate her, I hate her! I hate him, too! I hate them both! Why did I have to be born to THEM?" I sobbed.

I couldn't understand Mom's reaction at the time since she was constantly spewing out vitriolic verbiage about "the whore" to my two sisters and me whenever Dad wasn't home, which was almost all the time. And when he would return, she would hiss, "The bastard's home, be careful," and we would be filled with fear and tension. Later I realized her fear overrode her contempt for The Other Woman that day.

Not long after that, Dave presented me with a diamond engagement ring. It was beautiful, but I can't describe how dismayed I was. I didn't want to be going steady in the first place, and now I definitely did not want to be engaged. I loved him but didn't want to marry so young! But I didn't know how to hurt him with a refusal, since I really felt love for him. And the next thing I knew Dave and my mom were talking about a wedding date.

--
27

CHAPTER 7

So we had a beautiful, lavish wedding when I was 20. While engaged, I went to a doctor to learn about birth control before the wedding. But to my great consternation, I found I was pregnant three months after our wedding. I had a great figure and didn't want to lose it so early in our marriage.

And when I was feeling uncomfortably huge and awkward, my girlfriends took an exciting trip to New York City. How I envied them! I didn't want to be married so young let alone be pregnant. I wanted to be off on that adventure with them, not fat and pregnant.

But when at five months I felt movement in my womb, I was overwhelmed with love for this little baby growing inside me. And I had so much fun buying baby things. I even spent weeks learning how to crochet and laboring over my first ever crocheted project: a waffle patterned little jacket, hat and booties in pale turquoise, since I didn't know if our little baby was a boy or girl.

I had always wished I had an older brother, so I really wanted to have a boy first. But I remembered how awful I felt thinking Dad wanted a boy first. So I didn't tell anyone I wanted a boy, and I kept thinking of the baby as being a girl, so I wouldn't be disappointed if we didn't have a boy first.

During my eighth month of pregnancy, I stopped working at Corrections.

I eagerly read a book about natural childbirth and was convinced I would have an easy, relatively pain-free delivery, since I would be prepared and have no fear. What a crock! The labor was long and hard, and the pain intense. Labor was a total of 14 hours, nine of it continuous, severe, agonizing pain. I took nothing for the pain as I wanted to be alert for the birth. Was it a boy or a girl -- ? After many hours, I didn't know if it was night or day. During the first segment of pain I thought how I wanted to write the author of that natural childbirth book a letter telling him off.

What a relief when I managed the final push with the last bit of my diminishing strength, and out came our baby!!! Was it a boy or a girl -- ??

CHAPTER 8

THE HAPPY YEARS

A BOY! God gave us a boy! I was deliriously happy our firstborn was a boy. But I was very apprehensive as we took Steve home. I didn't even know what a little boy looked like until two weeks before he was born. I had never babysat and hadn't been around any babies so purposely visited someone with an infant boy. I was amazed how big the testicles looked. It was a good thing that I took a class for parenting, so I at least knew how to bathe and diaper Steve.

Poor little Steve cried a lot that first month. When I phoned Mom for advice, she kept telling me not to pick him up when he cried, or he would become spoiled. So poor Steve cried and cried. Thankfully there was an experienced mother in the apartment complex who explained Steve had colic. I was only able to nurse him for about two weeks, as he was a little chomper who gummed my poor nipples terribly raw and sore. He got colicky as we made the transition from breast milk to formula before we found one he could tolerate.

Fortunately Dave had taken the first weeks off work as we were both exhausted from lack of sleep. When he returned to work, I asked Mom if she could come for a couple of hours so I could take a nap. I was shocked when she refused saying, "You're married now and belong to his side of the family. Ask his mom." Dave's mom was very sweet but she didn't understand English, and I didn't understand or speak Chinese. I joked that because of that, we never had any arguments. But the truth was, it was an immense strain if we were together alone for even an hour, as we tried to communicate with hand gestures and a Chinese or English word here and there. So I struggled without much knowledge or sleep.

I often wondered later if Steve suffered from rejection in the womb those first four months before I felt him move and was flooded with love for him. And what about those hours he cried before our neighbor rescued him from our ignorance -- ? What harm did all of that do to his developing psyche?

Dave was a Bridge Design Engineer but drew up the blueprints and designed our home with the help of Joe, his good friend. Our new home was completed before Steve was born, but Dave's dad, who I dearly loved, died just before his birth. This dear old man had caught the bus and walked a few blocks to the apartment to visit me a couple of times during the day while I was pregnant. We were so sad he didn't have the joy of seeing his grandson. And Chinese superstition was that any household would have bad luck if we even crossed their threshold. So not only could we not move in or even enjoy viewing the inside of our new home, Mom kept us outside the door of their home and wouldn't let us inside! That fact and also her not wanting to answer my cry for help with Steve added to my feelings of rejection and abandonment. But Steve grew and thrived despite my inexperience.

Our sweet Laurie was born 16-1/2 months after Steve! Total labor was much shorter, so the intense pain was tolerable. It's often said that you don't remember the pain of childbirth, but I didn't find that true after Steve's birth. I hadn't been apprehensive going to the hospital to give birth to him, but I was very mindful of that painful agony with Steve while I was anticipating Laurie's birth.

We had decided that if it was another boy, we would try a third time for a girl. But we would stop if we had three boys. So what a relief and joy when it was only a few hours of hard labor and we learned we had a girl! One of each!!! Now we could stop at two, which was perfect for us, as each one could have their own bedroom. Immediately after giving birth, I was so happy I wrote Dave a love letter from my hospital bed before sleeping even though it was in the wee hours of the morning.

The years sped happily by. I cooked wonderful meals from scratch and practiced until I could bake light, flaky pie crusts, and I experimented with ingredients until my from-scratch apple pie was superb.

Steve and Laurie played happily together and didn't fight much at all. When Steve was around five, he announced when they grew up he was going to marry Laurie. He was angrily indignant when we told him he couldn't.

"W..h..y..y not?" he wailed!

"Well, when you're all grown up, you can marry her if you want. But believe me, you won't." was the answer I gave him which satisfied him.

And one time while playing monopoly my competitive spirit showed when I was gleefully winning and was going to force Laurie out of the game by taking all her money. Steve shamed me with his loving generosity. "I don't want Laurie to have to stop playing. Here, Laurie, take some of my money."

We had good neighborhood friends with kids the same age. And once or twice a month I taught all the children crafts.

Dave and I were deeply in love and enjoyed dancing the samba, rhumba, cha cha, waltz, foxtrot and swing together at the four dances we attended each year. And we went to San Francisco once or twice a year to attend live theater when the children were older and could have a sitter. Sex was so good we even stopped on the way home from SF to have sex in the car because we didn't want to wait until we got home.

Occasionally Dave would enjoy getting together with some guy friends to play poker. And I would have three gal friends come to our house to play Mahjongg while he was gone. But one day when he made plans and I called the three friends, I was shocked and hurt to discover they had already made plans with another woman who had invited them before I called to make up a foursome. After Dave left, and I had put the children to bed, I was suddenly overwhelmed with old feelings of rejection. All the old insecurity, abandonment emotions flooded over me, and I started weeping uncontrollably.

"God, I just want to be loved!" This pent-up cry from years of buried anguish burst forth from deep within me.

"I LOVE YOU!"

With that declaration, which seemed to resound and echo throughout the very core of my being, came an outpouring of liquid love from God so overwhelming, my anguished tears turned into sobs of joy and gratitude. For the first time in my life, I experienced pure, unconditional love, God's love. I cried for probably two hours as waves and waves of His healing love washed over me. I KNEW God was real! And I KNEW He loved ME! I truly felt love for EVERYONE and didn't have any bad feelings toward anyone.

When Dave returned, I eagerly told Dave about my experience, but he just said, "That's nice."

I just knew without anyone telling me I should start reading the Bible and pray. So that's what I did: Pray for half an hour and read the Bible for half an hour every day. The Holy Spirit didn't waste any time influencing my heart. And I insisted that we say grace before meals. Dave was reluctant but went along with the idea as long as I didn't expect him to pray. And I made sure we said grace when we occasionally dined out.

In addition I started looking for a Bible study. We had started attending a denominational church near our home soon after Steve was a toddler. I just felt like we should give him the benefit of Sunday school. Although that church didn't teach the gospel, I enjoyed the weekly meeting I attended where we discussed behavior in various situations.

Awhile later I told my close women friends about my "experience with God."

One friend said, "I knew something happened. You've changed. You won't even listen to gossip anymore."

Months went by and then at a dance, I saw a friend who came smiling toward my husband and me holding his date's hand. I had never met her before. I was absolutely stunned when, during the introduction, I heard her name and realized she was The Other Woman's Daughter. I nodded stiffly, and my husband and I turned and walked quickly away.

I was shocked at the intensity of the anger, resentment, and bitterness that surfaced. I didn't know all that was still buried within me. Memories returned of how when we were young, she had a horse and took dance and riding lessons while our family did without. I had forgiven her mother but discovered I hadn't forgiven her. Later I explained to my friend about his date's identity and why we had turned away. I felt smugly superior to her when he told me he wouldn't date her again. After awhile I was able to forgive again. I even phoned The Other Woman's Daughter to tell her I forgave her, but she didn't say a word.

Dave advanced at work and became a Bridge Design Engineer even without a college degree, and he designed the four-level interchange at Pomona, California. He was a wonderful provider and was even an excellent cook when he cooked occasionally. But about the eighth year of marriage, I realized we didn't have much in common except for a lot of passion and our great kids.

And although I had that wonderful experience with God, I was still hungering for love and acceptance. I enjoyed the attention I got from other men. I received validation from the approval in their eyes. I had vowed to myself as a teenager that I would never settle for a mediocre marriage.

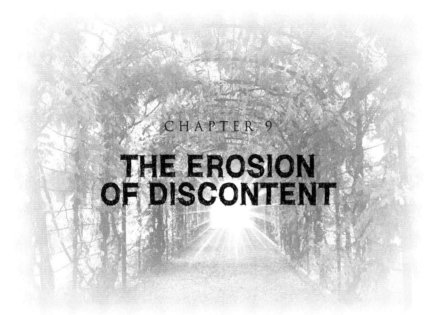

CHAPTER 9

THE EROSION
OF DISCONTENT

Dave just wasn't a communicator. He would be perfectly content to drive 90 miles to San Francisco and not say a word. And if we went to dinner alone and I attempted to make conversation, he would give the briefest of answers. Also when I wanted to discuss a movie we had just viewed, he would dismiss my attempts saying, "It's just a movie." So I would be sure we always went places with at least one other couple, so we would have enjoyable conversation while Dave remained a contented listener.

I know exactly what started tilting my thinking. I believed those terrible women's magazine articles saying you couldn't expect couples to stay together, since people grow at different rates and outgrow each other. And I was also influenced when I saw the movie Dr. Zhivago, which romanticized adultery. In that era, before that movie, adulterers were always punished by the end of the movie. But in that movie, it made you feel sorry for the lovers and you actually wanted them to get together. I started feeling as though I missed out by having known only one man intimately since I was a good, moral girl when I married Dave.

Also, in my early years, I read an article expressing that if you hadn't had much love growing up, you should love yourself more to make up for that lack. Without my realizing it, when I agreed with that notion, I opened the door for a selfish spirit to influence me.

And then an attractive bachelor started noticing me and complimenting me. He started fulfilling my emotional needs. I didn't realize it then, but according to the Five Languages of Love Test, Words of Affirmation and Meaningful Time Together were indications of love to me. For two years the bachelor would phone and say things like, "Wherever I go whatever I do, I think of you and wish we were together." We met for lunch once, but didn't touch.

I stopped saying grace because it felt hypocritical to do so, much to Dave's relief. I felt horrible. How could I think of another man during the day and then have great sex with my husband at night? But finally I couldn't stand the guilt any longer. I told the bachelor he needed to get on with his life, since he had stopped dating for those two years. But when he started dating younger women, I was tormented with jealousy. I was miserable when he did!

I confessed to Dave my emotional involvement with the bachelor. Dave told me he went to his office to confront him and how the bachelor had cowered. I was proud of Dave. For quite awhile Dave paid more attention to me and sex was even more frequent. It was better than our honeymoon.

By now, my reading the Bible time was shorter, and I was praying less and less and drifted away from God. And Dave went back to being engrossed in football and the stock market.

Awhile later a very gifted young artist with a gorgeous physique met me when I was at the YMCA pool with my children. I had worked hard at regaining my figure. He swam over to me and asked if I would go to his house someday so he could paint my portrait. I thought that was an original pick-up line but took his information out of curiosity.

I persuaded a woman friend to accompany me to his house, and we were both stunned at his artistry! Local critics gave him raves and he sold his first painting for over a thousand dollars when he was about 17. They predicted that if he fulfilled his potential, he would become "THE great artist of our generation" and compared his technique to famous painters.

Years later when I was single, we dated very briefly. That's when he told me he actually wanted to paint a nude portrait of me coming out of the sea when he first met me at the pool but was afraid to suggest that. He was right to not ask, as I never would have consented to posing without clothing.

And then when Steve and Laurie were in school full time, I tried volunteering weekly at a mental health outpatient clinic. There we served the patients cookies and tried to converse with them. But it was depressing to see them leave with so much hope, be returned to the same environment that often caused their condition, and then return to hospitalization again. So I stopped volunteering there.

I was trying to fill that void that only God could satisfy.

GOD AT WORK

Even though I didn't know it then, God has a plan for every life – a plan that will give you more joy and fulfillment than anything you could ever plan for yourself. After awhile, I saw a television program about ex-prisoners helping prisoners and how they needed volunteers. I always wanted to help people change for the better. But I didn't want to stuff envelopes and couldn't think of how else I could help there, so dismissed the idea as being implausible.

I was still attending a church that didn't explain about a personal relationship with God. I enjoyed trying to make newcomers feel at home. There I met a young woman who wanted to be a parole agent. I told her about the program I watched. I was amazed to learn her husband was the Director of that volunteer group in Sacramento! She urged me to meet him. I didn't know it at the time, but that was God arranging circumstances in my life!

So I started by being a volunteer secretary one day a week. The Director and staff would often leave me alone to man the office and tell me to lock the office when I left. Parolees would come in for coffee or to see the staff. So there I was with parolees who had committed crimes unknown to me…alone in an upstairs office at the end of a dark corridor. When it was 4 pm, I would shoo whoever was there out the door and lock up. Once I locked the door then realized I left a sweater inside. The parolee offered to "burgle the lock" to get me inside. But I told him that was what we were trying to reform him from. Now I realized God was protecting me while I was too trusting and not using good judgment.

Then when the Director invited me, I started going to the prison 45 miles away once a month with other volunteers for a pre-parole meeting. Ten to 20 volunteers and 50-100 inmates would attend. The inmates would predetermine themselves who to put on the "hot seat." He could say as little or as much as he wanted about himself and what he was going to do differently in the future. And we would question him and/or suggest options to unwise choices he was about to make to attempt to get his "head on straight" to avoid his returning to prison.

And once a week I also attended a post-release class where parolees would meet with "straight people" to talk over their problems. What was spoken here was privileged information not to leave the room.

One man at the post-release class had been an armed robber. He said he would literally salivate when he saw a Brinks armored truck because he wanted to rob it so much.

But he said, "I have my priorities straight and won't rob it cuz I don't want to return to the penitentiary."

But he finally admitted when we questioned him that he *would* rob it if he could get away with it. So he was still a thief at heart just controlling his behavior, waiting for an opportunity. I used to believe that psychology was the answer. Now I know psychology often helps us understand how we got to be as messed up as we are, but it's not the solution. It can help, but what we need is a new heart. And only God can give us a new heart.

Besides the pre and post release meetings, I also kept busy writing letters of encouragement to men incarcerated at that prison.

Despite being involved in all those activities, restlessness still persisted within me. More and more I felt dissatisfied that Dave and I didn't really have much in common. As I sat next to him watching football on television, I often wondered, "Why doesn't he notice I'm not turning the pages of this magazine or book I'm reading?"

While he was a wonderful, skillful lover and made a good income, money and sex aren't "where it's at." They only satisfied temporarily.

My marriage had deteriorated into the mediocrity I vowed I wouldn't tolerate.

MY WAYWARD YEARS

I decided to leave Dave after being married 15 years. It was really scary to contemplate supporting myself and Steve and Laurie. I struggled with making this decision for quite awhile. But I was selfish and had bought the premise that I was "missing out" by marrying so young.

Because my parents' unhappy marriage warped us, I didn't realize how harmful divorce would be to my children. I honestly thought being divorced was better for them than having parents who were unhappily married. And I believed the timing was good as Steve was 13. Later I learned that's the worst time for a teen's life to be disrupted, since he's still searching and insecure in his identity. The night we told them is a horrific memory.

We waited until we all had finished dinner.

"Steve and Laurie, we have something important to tell you," I began. "Sometimes people who are married change and aren't happy together like they first were. So we decided we need to live apart. But that doesn't change how we both feel about you. We'll both always love you. That will never change."

This scene is the second one indelibly imprinted on my mind. As I talked, Steve looked down at the table and squeezed the corn cob he had eaten over and over in his fist. Laurie was blinking back tears and picked one kernel of corn at a time and put it in her mouth and picked another kernel and so on and so on. She had never before eaten corn-on-the-cob in that manner.

I agreed to see a marriage counselor another couple recommended. He was really weird. My second session alone with him, he told me how he attended an Escalon retreat where everyone was naked and how free that felt. He said he put his head between a very heavy woman's huge nude breasts.

"It felt as though I was being swallowed by Mother Earth."

And he had me lie on the floor on my back and move my arms back and forth as though swimming.

I told him it cost too much and I wasn't returning. He told me he was writing a book and that I could type his manuscript there, and that would pay for my sessions. I told Dave I wasn't returning to this charlatan and how he behaved. Dave still wanted me to go and said, "He doesn't act like that with me." Didn't Dave see that this man was lecherous and lustful?

We decided to have the same attorney firm to save money since the divorce was amicable. The young attorney was sympathetic and comforting, so I went dancing with him when he asked. I didn't realize at the time it was unethical. When his partner heard about this impropriety, he took over and didn't represent me well.

I got the house with a large mortgage, an old car that needed to be replaced, and no alimony. Dave kept all the stocks and bonds, the new car, and all his retirement assets.

I quit the volunteer work and went back to being a secretary for Corrections, Youth Authority and Parole taking tests as soon as I

—

was eligible and advancing.

I started looking for love in all the wrong places, as the saying goes. I believed that it was permissible to have a "full relationship" as long as we were in love. So I was always "in love" with someone. I really believed at the time I did love each one. But now I realize although I really cared for each man, I was "in lust" not "in love." Several proposed marriage to me, but at the time marriage was not even a consideration for me. I was enjoying what I thought was the "new morality." Now I know there's no such thing. It's only the "old immorality."

But Gene was a special man in my life. He was a very gifted writer, and we enjoyed editing each other's writing, arguing about what needed to be deleted or revised. He knew and saw the worst of me and still loved me. However, my sense of self preservation prevented me from marrying him.

When he was a boy, his stepdad woke him at 5 am by throwing a glass of cold water on his face and booted him out the door, literally by the seat of his pants, to feed the livestock.

Gene went from crisis to crisis situation because of his wrong choices stemming from his need for acceptance and approval. An undependable friend asked to borrow his car.

Gene explained, "I told him I have a car problem and he needs to stay off the freeway and not go over 45 mph. I know he's going to speed on the freeway and ruin my engine. But if I don't lend him my car, word is going to get back to my friends that I don't help a friend in need." So against common sense and former experience, Gene lent the car to the jerk who did ruin the car. Gene couldn't afford to repair it, so he had to get up over an hour earlier to catch the bus to and from work. Gene later moved away to attend a technical school.

I wanted to shield my children so made certain I never had a man stay overnight and dated when the children were at their dad's.

I'm so glad God looks at our hearts and not what appears on the surface. He saw the hurting little mixed-up girl inside and had mercy on me and would be watching over me in the exciting adventures that were to come.

IT'S HARD
BEING A PIONEER

While I was secretary to the Chief of Parole Services, Corrections started hiring women as correctional officers. My intent was not to stay in uniform as an officer. It would be a stepping stone. I was very ambitious and always promoted as soon as I was eligible. This was the opportunity to combine work experience with education to promote to a counselor faster and then perhaps go up management.

I was among the first three women officers at the State prison California Men's Colony. It was really rough! Anytime you pioneer a new field, it's extremely difficult. Two of us were rooting for each other and felt whenever one of us did well, it was good for all of us. We tried to befriend the third woman, and I always praised her when she did well at the shooting range, etc. But she didn't want to be friends with either of us and was very competitive.

Many thought the other woman received job assignments in return for sexual favors. She also bragged about using her former welfare and husband's disability checks to go to Reno to gamble. Her husband was supposed to have a back problem yet bowled in a league. She also signed up for college courses that she didn't attend, and she received money from the State to purchase books. Then she kept the cash for the returned unread books.

At times I felt almost paranoid from the constant scrutiny by staff and inmates alike. Everyone seemed to know what job assignments we had and everything else about us.

Inmates at first didn't want us, some because of loss of privacy, while homosexuals considered us as rivals.

There were no uniforms made for women yet. We bought men's shirts and had to tailor them. We were given the color number and description of the fabric for the pants and had to make them ourselves. I didn't even realize how wide the belts were and all the equipment necessary to hang from the belts. So I had little tiny belt loops that were too small for the belt.

Staff had a legitimate concern because we were an unknown, unproven entity. No one knew if a woman officer would panic in an emergency. Initially women were only assigned to positions with limited contact with inmates: the Entrance Building, Visiting, Mail Room, Control, and Towers. This caused resentment in both the men and the women. Many males considered those assignments as desirable positions and sought after them. I considered them boring and wanted to interact with inmates.

I remember how apprehensive I was the night before we were to learn marksmanship. Never ever seeing a gun up close before, I imagined shooting myself in the hip or foot while taking the pistol out of the holster.

Amazingly I turned out to be one of the top marksmen in the whole prison and at the academy! And I don't know who was more astonished...the staff or me!

We didn't even go to the academy until I had worked there about four months. There were no women facilities there; so the women took turns guarding the bathroom door while we showered, etc., so no male would enter.

The day we had to qualify on the shooting range, it was pouring torrential sheets of rain. We stood, kneeled, and had to lie down on a muddy surface to shoot a 30-06 rifle, a pistol, and a shotgun. That rifle has such powerful recoil, if I wasn't firmly planted, it would have knocked me down. And it was so long and heavy for me, I had to lower it to chamber a round, heft it back up, shoot; down and up, up and down. I literally felt I was weight lifting. (Later the lighter mini 14 replaced the 30-06 rifle.) All, especially me, were amazed at my accuracy ability with the pistol and rifle. One Lieutenant called me Eagle Eyes!

We had to qualify once a year. Once I even shot all our target rounds in the little bull's eye with a pistol!

Initially the prison atmosphere was full of hate and anger. Officers would say how they wanted to retaliate the obnoxious behavior of inmates and described how they would. The air was filled with profanity, crude jokes, constant complaining from both inmates and staff. But because of women's demeanor, the atmosphere of the prison changed. Most inmates started acting like men instead of animals.

This was before sexual harassment laws were in effect, but I warded off unwanted advances with humor and just didn't respond if the jokes were too crude. So staff soon treated me with respect.

However a sergeant told me not to jog in shorts. I protested that it was during my off-duty time, it was summer, it was in my neighborhood, and the shorts weren't ultra short. But it was intimated that if I continued, it would hinder my advancement. I don't know who saw and reported me.

About 18 months after the women arrived at CMC, we were assigned to buildings. My duties were to lock the men in their cells for the night and then later make counts during the night. The fatherly sergeant seemed almost reluctant to leave me alone on the midnight shift where I was to oversee the 300 inmates alone. Each housing unit had three floors with a desk at each center foyer and a wing on each side housing 50 cells, a total of six wings. Inmates could use little mirrors and hold them in a position to watch your every movement in the foyer. (Years later there would be two officers and around 500 inmates in a building.)

I really wasn't concerned about danger and wasn't afraid of the assignment. But the eerie night sounds the creaking old buildings made caused me some discomfort. The officers in a nearby gun tower hung the wet mop outside to dry. And the occasional loud whacking sound of the wind slapping the mop against the wall made me jump. After I learned the origin of the sound, I eventually grew accustomed to it.

However, during my periodic checks on the cells, I never did get used to seeing an occasional large, muscular, homely man grin crazily at me with dark red lipstick smeared on his lips.

And I did learn to dread working the night shift in the building housing mentally disturbed inmates. One inmate would howl loudly during nights with full moons. Another inmate would hide naked so I would have to reluctantly search his cell with a flashlight knowing in what state I would find him. And it made me uncomfortable to see another agitated inmate pacing unceasingly all night long mumbling incoherently.

And one night after lights were out and the hallway was almost dark, an inmate taped a humongous insect spread eagled on his window hoping to elicit a shriek from me. It was ghastly startling to be doing a mundane security check only to spotlight this ugly spectacle in the dark! Thankfully I didn't scream in surprise. Otherwise there probably would have been at least six cell windows adorned with hideous insects the next night.

One huge man stood by his door and glared menacingly at me through his window at count time each night when I first was assigned to his building. So one night when he appeared as usual, I feigned great trepidation and horror and exclaimed, "Oh, Mr. Jones, you look SO fierce!" He cracked up laughing and would smile and wave at me after that.

And there were some dreadful nights at the prison. On the midnight watch, we had to be sure there was a live inmate in that room. We had to see living, breathing flesh. When I was assigned to a new building, I could tell how well the previous officer did his job by how the inmates slept. When they were counted correctly, the inmates trained themselves to sleep with an arm or leg sticking out while the rest of their bodies and limbs were covered by the blankets on cold nights.

When they were totally under the blanket and fell asleep with their earphones on, they couldn't hear my light tap on their cell door window. So I had to tap louder and louder. At times the rest of the wing would wake and scream obscenities.

"You f___ing bitch! I'd like to take a broom and stick it up your ass!" They knew I couldn't tell from which cells these insulting profanities were originating. It was hard not to allow their hate to hurt my feelings, but I managed to not show any emotion.

The inmates complained about my waking them up to the sergeant the next day. They didn't get mad at the inmates under the blankets with their headsets on; they got mad at me instead. After work the second night in one such building, I was appalled when the day sergeant suggested I could assume an inmate was under the blanket instead of waking him. I recounted to him how an inmate had escaped before and wasn't detected because he had hidden a dummy made of clothing in his place. I explained I didn't want my lack of diligence to cause an escape to go undetected.

I was disgusted to learn the third night they had assigned me to another quad. I felt I was being punished for doing my job. But that night, the really nice lieutenant came to my building. He wanted to reassure me he was proud of me for doing my job well and would back me up all the way.

I learned that inmates loved the volunteers, but as soon as I put on the uniform, I was instantly The Man, The System, The Authority. I represented all they rebelled from and hated.

And there was an officer who worked only in towers for over 20 years except for one week in the plaza. He screamed at me in rage because the first watch officer purposely didn't keep the intercom wires neatly arranged on a ledge and told him I did that to annoy him! He towered over me with his face red and contorted with rage. He was very intimidating, and I dreaded having to go up those tower stairs.

"Oh my gosh, I'm sandwiched between two loony officers!"

Sometimes he allowed a vehicle to be parked in the sally port. Going up the stairs, I would be filled with dread anticipating his rage when I had to remind him not to allow that. On my watch, we didn't have a sally port officer, and the vehicle would obstruct the fire engines if they had to turn into the roadway between the buildings and fence. God knows his other cruel actions toward me. He even wrote obnoxious and insulting remarks about me in the official log book that didn't pertain to business.

Finally, even though I could have issued a complaint, I asked for a hearing with supervisors. When I saw there would be a sergeant and lieutenant from both watches and a program supervisor, six males including that officer and me, I asked for a union representative. The request was denied "because of the cost of overtime for all the 2nd watch staff." That ruling was against my rights, but I went along with it because I already felt intimidated.

They ignored the fact the official log book with insults was missing. He wasn't reprimanded for his yelling and other unprofessional conduct. They just said we had to get along or we both would be punished even though I hadn't done anything!

In retrospect I realize I should have pursued the matter, but I felt "ganged up on," and my spirit felt crushed, hopeless, and defeated after being treated so unfairly in that meeting. It was truly an example of "the old boys' club," which I denied existed until that episode.

And there was an old sergeant in Control on the midnight shift who was known to often drink before work. He would mumble and then yell at me when I asked him what he said or asked a necessary question. Finally on the third night, I yelled back, "Look, Sergeant, we'd get along if you'd stop yelling. I'M NOT AN INMATE, I'M NOT A GREEN RECRUIT, AND I'M NOT YOUR WIFE! SO DON'T YELL AT ME!" The shocked look on his face almost made me laugh. And he never yelled at me again.

At times it was very difficult with all that negativity, but nevertheless, God started revealing His love to me in surprising ways.

CHAPTER 13

Divine Appointments

N o one I met ever talked about God at the prison that first year. But from my very first week at the prison, everywhere I went outside of work: at college, in a restaurant, on an airplane -- everywhere I went, people who seemed to really *know* Jesus and were *excited* about Him were talking to me about Him. I always liked to hear about God, even as a little girl. But when the conversation turned to anything personal like making a decision for Him, I'd get uncomfortable and change the subject or walk away.

You see, I had been running away from God. Because I had such a bad father image, I thought God was this huge Being in the sky with a lightning bolt ready to zap you if you get out of line. I thought giving my life totally to Him would be dull, difficult, too hard, and no fun. I was living for pleasure and enjoying it!

This sounds terrible, but I thought Christianity was for old people or losers who didn't have anything else going for them. I even thought that I would enjoy life and then surrender to Him in my 80's and slip into heaven before I died. I didn't think then about all those who die suddenly without a chance to even think about

—

God before crashing into eternity. And I thought I was a Christian who just hadn't given my will over to Him. After all, I still prayed, didn't I?

Then I heard about a gathering of Christians at a popular restaurant once a month from 10 am to 4 pm. "Well, I've dated all these heathens, wonder what dating a Christian guy is like? Well, God, I'm going for the wrong reasons. You already know that so I might as well be honest. Maybe I'll find someone good looking to date there."

My eyes took one full sweep of the room in a glance. "Well, God, I guess he's not here."

But the speaker's message made an impression on me. She explained once you pray about something, you're not to worry anymore but trust God instead. That was a revelation to me. I thought it was my duty to help God by worrying.

The next month I went to that meeting for the right reason: To learn more about God. After the group finished singing some worship choruses, they simultaneously, spontaneously started singing different songs in different languages. And it was unearthly beautiful! The knowledge that it had to be God gave me chills. I realized two people can't each decide to sing his own song without it sounding harsh and dissonant. He was making His presence known in this room. I knew I wanted to do this someday…. but not yet. I wasn't ready to give up my fun, immoral lifestyle. "There is pleasure in sin for a season," I later learned is written in the Bible.

"What is this? How can you do this?" I asked.

"It's singing in tongues."

"What's that?

"It's singing in the Spirit?"

"Well, what's that?" No one gave me an answer.

But I *did* pray, "God, will you please help me want to want to want Your will in my life." At that point I didn't even want to want to give my will to God.

At this time I had been working for over two months with Mac, a really nice older officer. We had long conversations, both fun and serious. Finally I confided to him I felt drawn to God. Then he shocked me!

"I've been a Christian for a long time." he told me with excitement. "I became a Christian when I was young, then I was widowed and got very lonely. So I went to a bar and met this woman that I started dating and really liked. But soon I was miserable, because I wanted to go back to God but didn't want to lose her. How can I tell this lady I met in a bar who likes to drink that I want to go to church every Sunday? Finally I told her and was amazed when she wanted to go with me. The first time we went, she went to the altar, got saved, and now she's really into God more than me!" So he started talking to me every night about God.

I even got to meet his wife Shirley at an officer's funeral awhile later. But we were just introduced and that was about it. But it was enough for Shirley, I was to later learn.

And one night when I was in the gun tower overlooking the entrance sally port, a group from church went in to sing. I always would lean out the window to welcome visiting groups and thank them when they left. This group had been in before. But this time on their way out, while the gate was closing behind them, and they were waiting for the Entrance Building door to open, they started singing a beautiful Christian chorus to me. They must have planned this in advance with the Christian sergeant, because he didn't open the door right away. Tears came to my eyes as I felt their love and God's love.

Finally I realized these weren't chance encounters. These were Divine Appointments. My concept of God was so distorted, it startled me to realize He was powerful enough to cause peoples' paths to cross. And I was thrilled that He cared enough to do that for ME! It finally dawned on me that He had a plan for my life, and it was better than anything I could plan for myself. But I knew giving my will meant giving up my birth control pills, giving Him control of my checkbook, and marrying who He wanted for me. That was a big decision.

At that time I was casually dating the news anchor man of a Santa Barbara television station.

"I'm feeling an attraction to God," I hesitantly told him.

"Well I hope you don't go THAT way!" was his response.

We had made a tentative date for that Friday, and he was going to call me Wednesday to set it. I heard about an outdoor Christian concert and felt inside I should attend. I knew if I chose the concert over our date, he wouldn't ask me out again. And that's what happened.

The cold wind from the ocean chilled me to the bone. I joined some friendly young girls and sat on the cushion I brought. I felt more and more uncomfortable: I was shivering from the nippy air; those attending were all younger than me; and the music was too loud and not to my liking. Several times I wanted to leave but something kept making me feel I should stay.

Then the leader of the group stepped to the microphone. "I very seldom give my testimony, but I feel I should give it tonight." And as he talked, tears poured down my face. He told about being on drugs, wanting girls, fame and riches. He sounded so much like my son. After he finished I asked if I could purchase a recording of his testimony for my son to hear.

"Oh, no, I could never record it. My dad is a famous actor and would get really upset if he heard I ever took drugs. I don't know why, but I feel I should tell you who my dad is," and then he did.

Astounded, I exclaimed, "My mom went to school with your

dad! I swam in your pool in the Hollywood Hills with my kids, and your mom pointed out the little building near the pool where your band practiced. It's not an accident you came here from Hollywood and gave your testimony tonight!"

He told me his mom gave her life to Jesus recently. That really impacted me. She was beautiful, had starred in a movie, had everything one could want, and surrendered to God while she was still fairly young.

So that night while kneeling alone by my bed, I surrendered to His love. His love took away my fear of His will for my life. I was disappointed I didn't feel His Presence or any emotion like I had so many years ago. It was just a matter of fact transaction.

I was working the midnight shift and intended to sleep 9 am til 4 pm. My plan was to go to the town plaza where their band was going to play and buy dinner there as it was a Holiday weekend. But I woke at 11 am and couldn't go back to sleep.

"Well, I'll go and have lunch there and go back to sleep before work," I thought.

I parked about eight blocks away, and there were several ways I could get to the plaza. God directed my steps, and five blocks away, there he was with his band leaving to return to Hollywood. I would have missed seeing him with my original plan.

"Wow, God arranged this!"

I ran up to him and purposely said, "Praise the Lord!" for the first time in my life. That phrase so foreign to my lips sounded very strange to my ears coming out of *me!* So I had the joy of telling him how his testimony helped me give my life to Jesus.

Walking with the Lord, I was learning, isn't following a bunch or rules and regulations trying to earn your way to heaven. It's a love relationship with Jesus. When I learned about His love for me, I just wanted to love Him back. I didn't HAVE to do the right things. I WANTED to!

But I realized I didn't really know how to love God. My love was conditional. You love me, and I'll love you. But you hurt me and watch how quickly I withdraw to protect myself or lash back in anger. I started asking God to teach me how to love Him. And soon at church when we started singing, I felt all this love and gratitude well up inside of me. I felt like I wanted to reach up and hug Him! And all these years later, I still feel the same.

God gave me so much joy and I was so excited to know God loved and forgave me, I couldn't stop talking about Him. The very first time was scary, though, when I told several at a party I had surrendered my will to God. It was like climbing out on a limb and cutting it off behind me. Once I spoke up, that meant I had to live it and not turn back. But when I told them and saw their positive reaction and interest, it encouraged me to tell others. In fact, one later went to church with me and gave her life to Jesus.

Before I opened my heart to Him, working at the prison was horrible! Officers and inmates alike were negative and complaining, and the atmosphere was filled with hate, gloom, and despair. I wanted to quit but didn't want to admit to failure. But after I gave my heart to Jesus, I realized: It's not an accident that I'm here. There's a purpose for my being here.

It was still scary though and I wondered how my life at the prison would change.

A Strange New Me

Mac was so happy when I told him I was now a Christian. Then he told me God brought my face before Shirley every day while she was under her hair dryer, and she would pray in tongues for me. I was astounded. But instead of being elated, pride made me feel insulted. "What did Mac tell her that made her think I was so bad off I needed prayer?" I wondered.

I didn't realize then that God often has His believers pray for many people they casually meet. Later I would often pray for transients hitch hiking realizing I might be the only person to pray for that man.

But right away I felt this huge burden of responsibility. I was the first Christian among ALL my friends, family, and fellow workers except for Mac that I knew about. I didn't know there were undercover Christian officers there.

"If it was up to me, they'll never get saved!" I mourned. "I don't know enough and I'm not a good enough example. They'll never come to Jesus!"

CHAPTER 14

Then within two weeks, as a brand new babe, Holy Spirit sweetly had me come across John 15: 4, 5: *I am the vine, you are the branches: He that abides in me, and I in him, the same brings forth much fruit: for without me you can do nothing.*

"That's it! I don't have to do anything. I can't! It's not my job. It's God's job. All I have to do is enjoy what I'm already doing: Walk and talk with Him, sing to Him, pray, read my Bible, and go to church and just enjoy His presence. And He'll do the rest." I'm so glad God took all that pressure off me by giving me that understanding early. My feeling of relief was like a deep, tranquil lake.

Now I wanted my own heavenly prayer language. My desiring to pray in tongues was another indication that I was really changed. I went forward to receive this phenomenon at two Christian gatherings. They prayed and then told me to open my mouth and speak in my new language. But my brain kept telling me, "They're waiting for you; you're disappointing them; I don't hear anything to say; I'm not going to fake this." I was to learn later, "The carnal (flesh) mind is an enemy to God." I was disappointed and wondered what was wrong with me since God didn't give this to me. I kept asking God for my language.

Then at 3:50 am when I was all alone in a gun tower, a three week-old Christian, Holy Spirit gave me my own special prayer language. I found I could be alert and vigilant and still pray and talk to God. I was asking for this, when inside I felt to just open my mouth and let strange sounds come forth so I did. I was disappointed that I didn't have a spectacular experience like some did. I started praying in tongues in just a matter of fact way with no emotion. But I was still happily praying away in my beautiful language which sounded like Polynesian to me. We had an hourly roll call of the towers to ensure we were all awake and not injured and unconscious.. I was concerned because I had heard some individuals couldn't talk in English for hours. The Holy Spirit is a gentleman and allowed me to speak in English for the roll call. And

I was relieved I could return to praying in tongues.

Soon, out of that love relationship, people started being drawn to want what I had. God gave me the joy and privilege of leading my best friend Gene to the Lord when I was a three-week old Christian. I was so new at this I wanted to be sure to do it right so had him repeat after me the prayer in a Christian magazine.

About three years later, when I received the message that Bill called to say Gene died, I said, "No, *Gene* called to say *Bill* died." When I called the number and learned Gene died of diabetes, I was stunned.

"God?! , You said You would use Gene in a way more glorious than I could imagine! But I know it's not Your fault. You did all You could. Why did he have to move away when I was a baby Christian? I didn't know how to help him receive the Baptism of the Holy Spirit then! Did he stay a Christian? Did he make it to heaven?"

God lovingly gave me a vision. I saw Gene in a gorgeous setting. He said, "Whee, Honey, I didn't know it would be this good here!" And he did cartwheels, which was totally out of character for him in the natural. What a wonderful reunion we'll have one day.

Because God used strangers to talk to me, the sincere prayer of my heart was, "God, I want to be a part of Your Divine Appointments to show people Your Love, like You did for me."

And it's been exciting, almost daily adventures with Him, everywhere I go. On airplanes, on trains, in restaurants, at stores, I meet hurting people and explain how God loves them and wants to forgive them and help them, and they pray with me. -- From tough bikers to little children.

For instance, I'd want to go to Gottschalk right after work but forget. Then I'd have to make a special trip after dinner. But unknown to me it was so that the store would be empty, and God could give me the words to show His love to a saleswoman. And after she got saved, she told me her boyfriend was a Christian but didn't know how to explain it to her as I did.

I returned another night. And again there were no customers. This time she received her prayer language.

And God changed my neighborhood by giving new life with Jesus to four children and four adults in four families. He gives me opportunities to talk to them by bringing over pizza to one family and giving the teens in another family rides to work. When two boys received their prayer language, they leaned their heads back on the sofa seemingly transported to another realm as they quietly prayed in tongues.

Amazingly the job I once hated became a joy. I realized: There's a purpose for my being here. And I prayed, "Lord prepare the people's minds and hearts. Bring them to me or me to them. And let me step aside and allow You to speak through me."

And when He brought inmates to me, He enabled me to *not* see them the way they are. In mass, they can be terrible. But when it was one on one, He helped me see them the way they could be. – The way Jesus wanted them to be. And inmates and staff started responding to His love in me flowing out to them.

I explained how Jesus can take away their pain and change their lives. And I pray with them one by one, and watch Jesus transform hard, cynical, bitter inmates and staff into tender, compassionate individuals. God loves them so much and knows what happened in their lives to cause them to be that way.

Sometimes He touched as many as eight, one by one, in one day! Usually two a week experience His transforming power. Staff would remark, "Something happened to that no-good son of a bitch!"

One lieutenant surprised me by leaning across his desk to shake my hand and tell me, "I'm glad you'll be in my unit for awhile."

At first my son and daughter and parents all thought I went weird. It took many years, but I had the joy and privilege of leading my daughter and Mom and Dad, one by one, to Jesus. What a wonder to watch Him heal their marriage. My son went through difficult years of rebellion, but now he's a Christian, too. He has faithfully worked with the sound system and recording equipment at his church for many years. My daughter goes on two-week mission trips to foreign countries every year.

Another major concept God gave me early was to praise God IN SPITE OF not FOR your circumstances. This habit would sustain me and be invaluable while going through the events to come.

And I was also learning: God was taking out my wrong desires and putting His desires in me! For it is God which worketh in you both to will and to do of His good pleasure. Phil. 2:13 KJV. And another translation: For it is God who in His good will is at work in your hearts, inspiring your will and your actions. Gspd, An American Translation (E. J. Goodspeed)

Behind each salvation is a wonderful story. Some are more amazing than others.

CHAPTER 15

Divine Protection and Alertness

The inmates were mostly cooperative and responded well to my treating them with respect and courtesy. And I would take the time to explain why certain rules were necessary.

For instance many inmates would play their radios loudly while the ruling was to always use earphones while inside the building. That happened so frequently I typed out a written warning with the explanation:

"This is a warning. The next time you have your radio on without using earphones, you will receive a 115. There are men who sleep odd hours who have to work at 4 am." The inmates then complied without complaining. (A 115 is a disciplinary report.)

Several inmates told me that never had occurred to them. One actually thought that rule was just to harass them and cause them more misery.

CHAPTER 15

Rescued!

I was among the very first women to work the buildings day shift. The men have their own keys to their cells. They come and go from their cells to work, school, or free time in the yard. On day shift each building officer supervised a floor with 100 inmates.

Occasionally an inmate will react angrily if they are refused something they want or are corrected. That happened when I was both a new Christian and also new to working days in a building. A huge inmate with a menacing attitude was belligerent at first. Then his anger was rapidly escalating while I was praying under my breath for wisdom and asking God to show me how to defuse the situation. Just as his anger was about to reach the boiling point and I was starting to be alarmed, God had a bigger inmate walk up.

"Hey," his voice boomed, "You don't mess with Officer Honey. She walks with God!" As he glared at him, the once-menacing inmate backed off and disappeared!

I thanked my rescuer gratefully, and he just smiled and went on his way. Later I looked through all 300 photos of the inmates on all three floors but couldn't find his photo. Later I wondered: Was he an angel? The Bible says we entertain angels unaware -- !

Escape Deterred!

One time I was working a gun tower on the evening shift. I heard an officer radio, "An inmate's on the maintenance roof!"

Immediately, I swung my roof spotlight that direction and spotted an inmate running on the roof towards me! I grabbed my rifle, chambered a round, and pointed it out the window at him in one smooth motion. At the same time I yelled,

"Stop! Or I'll shoot!"

He heard the loud, metallic sound in the quiet night of the

70

round going into firing position, and he swung himself over the edge of the roof with his fingertips on the roof and then let go!

I advised on the radio, "The inmate jumped off the roof behind the building in back of the family visiting trailer by C Quad!"

Then on the radio to the West Outside Patrol who was coming out of the nearby Fire House, I commanded, "West OP, swing your car around and point your headlights toward the fence by Building 6. The inmate might try for the fence!"

I held my rifle out the window ready to fire if necessary. I wondered if he had it planned and had earlier prepared something soft for him to land on. I was also answering the Watch Lieutenant's questions on the radio.

Just then the East Outside Patrol Officer, who apparently wasn't paying attention to the radio transmissions, drove up to the truck sally port gate and tooted his horn to open the gate. He wanted to bring the outside visitor in for a family visit! When I didn't open the gate, he tooted his horn again and called out his window, "What's the matter? Are you asleep?" -- !

He didn't even notice the weapon I had sticking out the window, my tower spotlight on, nor the other car pointed toward the fence. I called out the window, "There's an escape attempt going on right now! I'm not going to open up the gate."

Officers from the Plaza soon arrived and found the inmate on the ground out of my vision with a broken hip and legs.

I always wondered before how I would handle an emergency, because you never know until it happens. It surprised me how calm and efficient I had been. But I started shaking from the adrenaline rush soon after while I was writing out the incident report. All during the incident I had been praying in tongues between radio reports.

Another time God also had me look just at the right instant

to spot an inmate ducking into a trailer of a truck parked in the maintenance corridor preventing another escape. It happened so fast, my mind even questioned if that's what I actually saw and how embarrassed I would be if I had imagined it. But I reported it, and the inmate was found.

Serious Injury Prevented

And once I was again temporarily assigned to work in a gun tower. All the steps and railings are metal inside the towers. The first two flights are like normal steps, and the third flight is like a step ladder. One day as I was leaving the tower, instead of facing the steps and backing down, I faced the other way and started walking down the ladder steps since I was holding things in both hands so couldn't use the handrail. I was wearing new shoes with slippery soles. Suddenly my foot slid, and I was hurtling head first down the metal stairs!

I screamed, "Help me, Jesus!!!" Instantly I found my fall had stopped, and I was upside down holding onto the handrail! One foot had somehow become entwined around the railing stopping my headlong descent. As I was loudly praising God and thanking Jesus, I saw the scared face of my relief officer who came down the steps to help disentangle me from the handrail. He witnessed my fall as he had been in the process of closing the trap door behind me. He was pale and shaking while I was jubilant!

I had wondered before: If I was ever in an emergency situation, would my first thought be to call out to the Lord? And now I knew. I *know* an angel must have intervened. There was no way I could have ended upside down holding onto the handrail on the right with my foot in that position on that same handrail when I was walking down the center of the steps. My head would have normally banged on the center of the metal stairs as I tumbled all the way down.

Warning Ignored

Unfortunately, many officers had the misguided opinion that Christians are too trusting and gullible. They didn't realize that the Lord gives His believers wisdom, warns them, and keeps them alert. By his grace I found hidden contraband and overheard inmates planning and was able to prevent their visitor from bringing in drugs.

But one time I didn't heed God's warning. Dining Room Officer was one of my least desirable assignments. So much could go wrong. Responsibilities included hiring and firing two crews for both dining rooms in the quad, checking the menu and making certain if there was food to be fried, have the fry cooks arrive on time, coffee was started on time, utensils on the table along with salt and pepper and filled water pitchers. Food had to be flowing on time from the heated food carts from the kitchen to the feeding line before serving pans were empty. Clean-up crews had to do a good job. Another concern was prevention of food being smuggled out.

One day I was with about 40 inmates waiting for the count of inmates to clear so we could serve breakfast. I had forgotten to have sugar out, and the inmates were griping about having to drink their unsweetened coffee. And I also missed sugar in my coffee. I was new to this assignment and thought the locked pantry was small enough that I could reach the sugar from the doorway.

To my dismay, the pantry was larger than I remembered. It would take five steps to reach the sugar. I felt inside an inward caution not to do it. But the inmates and I wanted sugar. I ignored the warning and stepped inside, grabbed the sugar, turned around and was startled to see an inmate inside the pantry with both arms outstretched toward me!

In my most commanding tone I ordered, "Don't you take one more step toward me or I'll push this alarm and they'll take you away!"

As he backed away I vowed to myself, "God, with Your help, I won't ignore Your warning again. Thank You for protecting me!"

Guidance from God

When I worked the midnight shift in the buildings, some inmates would ask me to stop by their cells later to talk. I depended on God to show me which ones were sincere.

"God, have him be asleep and if I'm to talk to him, have him wake with just one sweep of the flashlight on the ceiling."

Using this method, God had me talk to several. One was Russ who I talked to about God for about half an hour two nights in a row. But the third night, he didn't wake up. I even flashed the light on his sleeping face, and he didn't wake up. I apologized to God for trying to wake him up so I could witness some more to him.

The next morning at the end of my shift and as Russ was leaving for work, he asked, "Why didn't you come by to talk last night?"

"You'd better check out your motivation because God didn't want me to talk to you," was my quick retort.

I went to my next assignment and returned to that building about three months later. Russ prayed with me and gave Jesus his life at that time. Then he confessed,

"I was curious about God the first two times you talked to me. But the third time I wasn't interested in God and just wanted you to stand by my door so I could get aroused and jack off later. I thought, 'Wow, God told her about my intentions,' and realized God is real."

Shocked, I answered, "Well, God didn't tell me THAT, but He did show me not to talk to you that night!"

Another time while I was working days, an inmate said, "I just became a Christian and was transferred here soon after. I don't know any Christians here. Could you please help me?" He looked really sincere as he pleaded.

I prayed in tongues under my breath, then answered, "I don't feel God wants me to talk to you. Maybe it's because you're not sincere. But if you are, don't worry what I or anyone else thinks. Just be concerned about pleasing God." With that said, I walked away.

Later I worried, "That was such a harsh thing to say if he really was a brand new Christian. And I said it right in front of his friend sitting nearby."

Very soon I was monitoring phone conversations when that same inmate called a homosexual and manipulated him.

"It's below freezing here and I don't have warm clothes. Send me a Pendleton jacket. Also we don't have TV or movies. Could you send me a cassette player? Not a cheap one, a good one, an expensive one."

What a pack of lies. Our evenings were warm, they are issued jackets, and they also have both TV and movies. If I had talked to him about the Lord, both he and his friend would have had a hearty laugh at my expense. God was watching out for me.

No Earthly Promotion

Although it had been my intention to not stay an officer, I knew inside my heart that God wanted me not to take any tests to promote. I could be used to bring inmates and staff to Jesus as an officer, while promoting to supervisory positions would limit my sharing. As an officer I was right there when inmates were ready to hear about God after blowing up or after receiving sad news from home.

It hurt my pride to stay an officer, especially when even captains have asked me to take the test for sergeant. I knew I could pass the test. Then they would train me to become a lieutenant. I was a double minority. I was Asian and also a woman. That would look good on paper for Corrections Headquarters. And I knew I was sharper than many sergeants. I put those thoughts aside.

Occasionally during some assignments, I would walk the perimeter of the whole East side and on another, the whole West Facility. Each time during that perimeter check I would pray in tongues and declare in my heart for God Dt. 11:24: Every place whereon the soles of your feet shall tread shall be yours...

So in accordance, there were many additional exciting adventures awaiting me.

CHAPTER 16

God Adventures

Midway in my career, I began to feel that God wanted me to leave my comfortable assignment and request Vacation-Relief assignments. No way did I want to do that! I dreaded the thought of taking officers' assignments every two or three weeks when they went on vacation. That entailed working all over both the medium and minimum prisons, working miscellaneous jobs, varied hours and days off, and having different supervisors, officers, and inmates. East Facility has its own hospital, dining halls, education, and work areas. There, the hardened criminals are contained in cellblocks but have their own cell keys and move about. West Facility also has the same but in a more relaxed dormitory arrangement, where the inmates have more freedom.

I'm really not brave and felt dread and apprehension about going through the hassles of all those changes plus the insecurity and discomfort of always learning new duties and routines. That meant I had to be flexible with sleeping. Some assignments I would have to collect necessary equipment and be far into the interior of the prison by 4:30 am! The next job might start at 10 pm or 12 M or 7 am. But I always want to please Him and knew there is safety, peace, and joy only in the center of His will. So I told God, without much enthusiasm, that I'd do it but wanted to know for certain it was His will. About 20 minutes later an incredible joyful anticipation and excitement started bubbling up inside of me! So I submitted a request for that job change quickly before I chickened out. There were some pretty awful moments, but most of the time there were really joyful adventures.

The conversations start on many varied topics, and it's amazing how the Holy Spirit creates an opening and changes the topic. Here are a few examples of God's mercy, power, and love in action.

Missing Page

An inmate brought me a page lost from an address book. So I posted a note on the office window saying, "I have a page from an address book. It has the name Glendra. Identify other names from that page, and you can have it." Hours went by with no one claiming it. I thought to myself finally, "I'll stop the next man that goes by." Right then an inmate walked by. I called him over and asked him to read my note posted on the window and spread the word. He read the note and had a funny expression on his face as he left. Then he returned with his address book and told me the other names on the page.

So as I gave him the page, I explained it wasn't by chance that I stopped him because nothing happens in my life by accident. I asked about his spiritual background. He told me his dad was a Reverend. God gave me Word of Knowledge about his past and current situation. I told him God told me these things to show him how much He loves him. After some discussion and prayer, he quietly asked Jesus into his heart and surrendered his life.

The Shack

Another time an inmate came to ask about something. I asked, "Were you brought up in a wooden home?"

"No".

"I'm confused. I get the feeling you spent a lot of time in a wooden building."

"I can't believe you know that! How do you know that? I used to go to a wood shack near my house all the time!" he exclaimed.

I concluded, "And you were hiding from your dad, terrified, because he used to beat you."

As he gave an amazed nod, I explained God gave me supernatural knowledge about his life to show him God loves him and knows everything about him. Feeling touched in his heart, he prayed with me and gave his life to Jesus.

Ready and Waiting

And when I was on the yard, Brad was just chit chatting with me and Rich, another inmate. Out of the blue, I said,

"You need to give your life to Jesus so He can keep you out of prison."

Surprised, he said, "I've been seriously thinking I need to change."

After I explained, he received salvation and told Rich how good he felt. Right after he received Jesus, the sergeant called me over the radio. I told Brad to find me back out in the yard later because Jesus wanted to give him power to walk with Him.

Later in the yard, Brad called out to me. "I've got them all lined up for you." -- ! He had Rich and two others with him. I was amazed and excited about what God was going to do. We moved to a shady area where I could talk to them but still be looking toward the yard. They wanted to get me a bucket to sit on while they sat on the ground but I preferred to stand. They were very attentive. I explained the gospel again, and the other three got saved. Then I explained the Baptism of the Holy Spirit, and Jesus baptized all five of them! Two took awhile to receive, so I had to pray them through.

Almost immediately satan attacked Rich's mind. "My parents didn't say anything about this." I explained how satan will try to steal the language from them. He wanted to lead them around by the carnal mind, which is an enemy against God, and the carnal mind will actually try to take them to hell until the day they die. So he decided to continue to pray in tongues.

Officer's Approval

While working outside as the yard officer, I started talking to David, a Christian, and saw Francisco listening with longing in his heart. So I explained the gospel to Francisco. I wanted a more private place so took them over to the side of a nice officer's dorm to explain the BHS and to pray for them loud enough for the officer inside to hear through his open window. The officer came to the window and gave me an approving sign as both inmates received their new language, even though the officer hadn't received his yet.

Through Rain and Sleet

While I worked on West, one assignment was to escort trucks into the prison, stay with them, and then escort them out after their delivery. Once a week for two weeks I talked to a Swacky Farm driver about God. He was really interested and said he used to be a Christian. He said he wanted to talk more on his next trip. I explained I might not be the officer to escort him in next week. All that week I prayed for him off and on.

Then the day he was to come in again, I awoke with a bad sore throat. And it was really stormy. I knew I would get drenched even with my rain gear. I was really tempted to stay home on sick leave.

"God, I don't want to work unless You have me be the escort officer for that driver. Should I go in to work or stay home sick?"

I felt in my heart I should go to work in that storm.

Sure enough I was drenched and cold most of the time. I kept praying that God would time Swacky Farm to come when I would be available between other truck escorts, and He did. And before he left, I had the driver go with me into the little office below the sally port tower officer to pray. I had talked to the officer above us about the Lord before, and I wanted him to hear the driver give his heart to Jesus. He got very emotional as he felt Jesus come into his heart, and I was glad the tower officer heard him.

God's Power in the Library

Some encounters are quite dramatic. When I was Library Officer, one of my workers told me he needed to be set free from something. I felt it was sexual perversion of some kind. So I told him to fast all day, and I would pray for him before the library closed. He fasted all the next day. Usually I have to scoot the men out the door near my shift's completion. But this night, without any prompting on my part, all the inmates left 45 minutes early! So I dismissed my other workers.

After I prepared his heart with scriptures, I started rebuking demonic spirits, and he fell to the floor under the power of God and started screaming really loudly! I always leave the door open so no one can ever accuse me of doing anything improper. As he was screaming, I prayed, "Oh God, close the people's ears nearby, have no one hear him, and have no one come in to disturb us." And even though I could see people walking right past the library door, no one heard this man's loud screams! And after a while, he got up, elated, delivered, free, and praying in tongues for the first time.

—

What an awesome God we have!

Tennessee's Song

Tennessee came to the dorm I was working to repair a leaking faucet in the staff restroom. While he worked, I learned he's called to be an evangelist and God gives him songs. I explained about the Baptism of the Holy Spirit, and he received his language.

Awhile later he told me, "I had a dream last night. I dreamed I fell down a hole. I looked up and could see people passing. I yelled for help. One man looked down and said, 'I can't help you. Only Jesus can.'

"So I asked Jesus to help me. The next thing I knew, I was out of the hole and in front of a large congregation. I was singing with a choir in back of me. And I was singing a song I never heard before. When I woke up, I wrote the lyrics and melody down."

And later Tennessee played his guitar and sang the song God gave him outside my office window so I could hear him. It was beautiful, and he had a great voice. How I wish I could have been able to record it!

Family Visit Surprise

One time I was working evening shift in a gun tower overlooking the yards and a family visiting trailer. The inmate phoned me about three times asking if the Outside Patrol Officer would bring him cigarettes. (Now there's no smoking in the whole institution. But back then, they could. The officer brought him cigarettes.)

I told him, "Jesus could free you from even the desire for cigarettes if you give your life to Him."

"That's what I need to do. That's what's I need to do."

I explained, prayed with him, and Jesus saved him. And after

I explained about the Baptism of the Holy Spirit he received his prayer language, too. He was shouting with excitement!

I explained, "When the urge to smoke comes, call out 'Help!' to Jesus. Then imagine Him inside of you getting bigger and let Him resist in you through you and for you."

When I called the trailer later to count him, his wife answered.

"Has he smoked a cigarette yet?"

"No. He took one out, looked at it, and put it away. And he's not mean and grouchy like he was earlier without smoking. And he's been reading the Bible they have in here."

"That's because he gave his life to Jesus and He's helping him not to smoke."

I explained more, and she also received salvation and the Baptism of the Holy Spirit over the phone as her husband had!

Now instead of only chasing her around the bed, they were both also reading the Bible and praying in tongues together!

Translator Touched

One day during lunch time I started talking to Peter at the door of the dorm. He looked like an ex-gang member. I learned he was a Christian who didn't know much about the baptism of the Holy Spirit. We decided to talk more after lunch. In the meantime God showed me my dorm porter Jose's heart was tender towards the Lord. I asked in Spanish, "Entiende usted Jesus Christo te ama usted? Jesus Christo quieres entrar su corazon y puede cambiar su vida -- dar usted vida nueva." (Do you know Jesus loves you? Jesus wants to enter your heart and change your life – give you a new life.)

After lunch I asked Peter to translate while I told Jose the gospel, and Jesus saved him! Then I explained the Baptism of the

Holy Spirit with Peter's help, and both received the Baptism of the Holy Spirit.

I know just enough Spanish to find out if an Hispanic is interested; and if so, then I get a translator. And a few times, God has had me purposely get an *unsaved* inmate to translate. And even though the unsaved translator would be uncomfortable and reluctant to translate, the Holy Spirit would touch them both, and Jesus would save both! And sometimes, both would also pray in tongues.

Just in Time

And God brought Tin, a young Asian, and I together. I asked him if he had any spiritual background. He said his mom is Buddhist and his dad is Catholic. He said he was thinking of becoming a Buddhist now. I explained the gospel, and he recommitted. Then he explained that I led him to salvation a few months ago in the yard when I worked evenings. So this time I had time to explain the BHS, and he received with joy. I also explained about the two natures, the new and the old, being in conflict with each other and how you have to feed one and starve the other; and how you have to feed your spiritual man soul food, the Bible. God put us together to give him another start before he let the Buddhist forces in.

Deliverance from Rage

Cecillio was saved and received the Baptism of the Holy Spirit when I was in his dorm about one year earlier but backslid. I knew he was backslid when I was in his dorm about six months earlier, but he avoided me. He had a bad temper and was always complaining about inmates and getting angry at the inmates or officers.

I had him paged when he didn't report for work. When he reported I started to correct him. He blew up saying, "I worked hard this morning for Inspection Day. I do my work. You don't have to call me over the loudspeaker. I quit!" and walked out of the office. I followed him telling him to come back to the office. When he ignored me, I told him, "You'd better think it over and come back to the office. If you don't, I'll give you a disciplinary report. Your bad temper is going to get you killed or send you back to prison." I knew he would come back. Sure enough he returned in a little while. I was stern with him and wouldn't allow him to finish when he kept trying to give excuses. I told him he needed to repent and give his heart back to Jesus because he's no match for the devil on his own, and that the devil would destroy his life and soul if he didn't.

I also explained through Word of Knowledge that God told me he was molested as a little boy and anger came in. I explained unforgiveness would destroy him, and Jesus could help him forgive. I explained that bitterness was like acid inside, and it was like drinking poison and hoping the perpetrator would die. He had tears in his eyes and agreed to recommit and forgive. Praise the Lord, he received Jesus with great joy. I gave him the teaching on the Baptism of the Holy Spirit, and he received with even more joy. As I rebuked the temper demon, he shook hard visibly, and he felt it leave as Jesus delivered him.

Rowdy Dorm

On one assignment the unit was locked down because of an incident. The inmates had to remain on their bunks, and I had a really rowdy dorm. I was standing in the middle of the dorm quieting the 90 men down, when a biker type said, "Give us a speech, Officer French. Come on!"

He was joking, but I started preaching: "I used to be a volunteer working with parolees. I came here because I want to help men change before they get outside, because it's so hard for some to reform later after they leave."

There were some loud catcalls and jibes. But the tough biker yelled, "Shut up! Let her talk."

I continued, "God loves you, and He can change you if you give your heart to Jesus. When you think about God now, you feel uncomfortable. You can't imagine how good it feels to have His peace, joy, and forgiveness instead of guilt, shame, or dread. The devil knows how to play us like puppets on a string. He knows what strings to pull to make us dance his tune. But God has a plan for the rest of your life. If you want to hear more, come see me in the office later."

As I walked away, the biker said, "She's got heart." Someone else said, "Let's give her a hand," and they clapped!

Several stopped by later to ask questions and talk. The biker stopped by four times in one day to listen a little at a time. I learned his wife is a Christian. I told him, "God really wants to answer your wife's prayers for you."

Jesus saved four and baptized seven men in that dorm during a three-week period. That first rough day I thought, "And to think I canceled my three-week vacation for this assignment. Maybe God wanted to spare me having to deal with these orangutans." But God turned it all for good, and it was worth the hardships for those souls to be touched.

Test of Faith

While at work at the prison, I injured my right forearm. The doctor at the prison confirmed what I thought: It was tenno syno vitis. The sheath lining of the tendon was injured. Any movement only irritated it more causing increased inflammation. It especially hurt to move my hand left to right or vice versa or to pull anything. It had occurred before. And when it was severe, even the motion of applying lipstick hurt.

The doctor told me to rest it for three days, use a wrist splint, take a muscle relaxer, and sent me home. I was assigned to an evening outdoor position, and I thought it would be nice to be out of the cold and relax at home and read a book.

Then I heard the Lord ask, "Would you rather stay home injured or go to work?"

What I really wanted to do was stay home AND be healed. But I realized the injury could progress and last a long time if I didn't go to work. I felt He wanted me to return to work the next day, leave the muscle relaxer pills and splint behind, and not baby that arm. I reluctantly informed the prison I was returning to work the next day.

As I was going out my front door the next morning I exclaimed, "God, I believe this is You telling me to go. I'm leaving the pills and splint behind. Stop me if it's not You!!!"

At work I thought, "It's not faith if I don't tell anyone." So I told one believer and two non Christians at work. They all warned me my arm could really get worse.

On that job I had to turn locks with huge keys and pull open large, heavy, metal gates -- all painful tasks with this injury. Each time I reached out with the keys purposely with my damaged right arm, I asked God whether I should praise Him for my healing or rebuke satan, and then do whichever He said. It hurt very much each time. And then about three or four hours after I started work, I turned a key, and there was no pain!! God healed my arm! It was quite a witness to the ones I told. Thank you, Jesus!

Womanizer Blindsided

I met Angel who is a black with a strip of hair shaved above his ears and long hair below the shaved strip. He thought he was a really cool dude. He was telling me how he was backslid and paroling soon and all the reasons he still wanted to sin and not recommit. He was going to go out and really party and womanize.

After we had talked awhile and I explained the only things God didn't want for him are things that are harmful, destructive, and could ultimately destroy him, he let me pray with him to ask God to help him want to want His will in his life.

He told me his dad is a pastor and his mom is an evangelist... how he was going to be sentenced to 60 years in prison and got on his knees and begged God to change the sentence. He plea bargained, and God did a miracle and reduced his sentence to 12 years, and he only served six!

I asked him, "Don't you feel ashamed that after God did that wonderful act of mercy for you, you just ignored Him? And how could you not surrender to a wonderful, powerful God of such love and grace?"

Then he said, "It's time, isn't it? It's time!" We both got happy and excited. He prayed with me and Jesus saved and baptized him in the Holy Spirit. He exclaimed, "I'm going to my cell and throw out all the pornography right away."

Better than Medication

Next I worked the quad housing mentally disturbed inmates. I had to handcuff and escort Chuck to see the psychiatrist. Afterward, as we talked, he told me he was born again, and that Jesus convicted him of taking medication. He had tears in his eyes and said, "I let Him down. I compromised. If I didn't take the meds, I would be housed in the crazy unit instead of staying in this quad."

I assured him he did what he had to do, that Jesus understood and didn't condemn him for that. Then I told him about the baptism in the Holy Spirit. At first he didn't think God wanted it for him. But after I gave him scriptures, he was eager to receive, and Jesus put the faith in his heart to believe he would receive. *He also said he hadn't been able to feel joy or sorrow for years.* But when Jesus baptized him, he felt *great* joy! We were sitting on the bleachers, and he started shaking and rocking and was praying really loudly in tongues.

A friend of his came by and asked, "Are you OK?"

"Yes, but please excuse us, I'm busy right now."

The friend looked doubtful and gave me a reproachful look commenting, "He was much calmer before."

But Chuck just ignored him because he was so-o-o happy. I cautioned him who to tell about tongues and not to pray loudly in tongues publicly. He agreed.

Months later on West, I was supposed to be the Yard Officer, but they assigned me to Dorm 7 instead. There an inmate came up to me and said, "I know who you are. You escorted Chuck. What you didn't know is this: Just the day before you two met, Chuck had said, 'Where's this joy Christians are supposed to have? Where's the joy?' And then the next day you helped him receive God's joy."

God could have put me anywhere and could have put this inmate anywhere. But this man had just transferred from East into this dorm two weeks earlier. God had our paths cross so that we could celebrate together what He's doing in Chuck's life.

Deliverance from Homosexuality

Ron was walking, and I joined him circling the yard. He was a handsome man in his twenties. As we talked, the conversation turned serious as he confided when he first arrived and was threatened of being gang raped, he accepted the protection offered by a large inmate who made him his "queen." He knew scriptures and wanted to be forgiven. So we sat on a bench, we prayed, and his eyes teared up as he felt Jesus' love and forgiveness. He stayed in his cell the few days remaining before he paroled. And months later, he wrote to his friends. He asked them to tell me he was doing well as a legal assistant and heterosexual.

While Ron looked masculine, Geri was a flamboyant homosexual who walked with mincing steps and made feminine gestures with his hands. When we talked, he dropped his caricature of being a woman. I could see the sadness in his eyes. Many, many talks later over a long period of time, Geri opened his heart and gave his life to Jesus. He sobbed with joy!

And as I usually do with new converts, I encouraged him to feed his soul man by reading the Bible, to pray, and attend chapel. And I told Christian inmates and officers in his area to encourage him. I often call the chapel and arrange for them to have a Bible ready for the man to pick up. And as God brings each to my mind from time to time, I pray for each one often.

More Divine Encounters

Book of Acts Encounter for Tyrone

One inmate with a spectacular build strode around near me without his shirt on. "Tell me, what's a nice woman like you working in a place like this?"

That sounded like a line from a grade C movie, and I had to restrain myself from laughing.

"Well, it might sound corny, but I like to help men change so they don't have to return to prison."

"You think you can change a man the short time you're here?" he jeered.

"I can't. But God can."

He gave a disgusted snort. "Oh, you're into religion like my mom."

"No, what I have isn't religion. I'm not following a bunch of

—

rules and regulations trying to earn my way to heaven. I have a love relationship with Jesus."

He disappeared only to return soon with his shirt on. He showed me the title of a book and turned it over quickly as he placed it on the podium.

"I don't want anyone here to see the title and think I read this kind of stuff. My mom sent it to me."

After we talked awhile, he let me pray with him. I prayed discreetly with my eyes open and touched his arm with one finger.

"God, help Tyrone to want to want to want to give his will to You."

After we talked more I could see God was changing him and asked for his permission then prayed,

"God please help Tyrone want to want to give his will to You."

Soon I asked, "If Jesus made Himself real to you, would you give Him your life?"

"Sure, if God was real. I'd be a fool not to!"

We talked more between my walking to check the two wings from time to time. And within an hour, Tyrone was ready and gave his heart to Jesus. He was beaming. He even turned the book over and showed the cover.

"Wow, Jesus is so proud of you! You're not ashamed of Him!"

I told him to go to his cell and think about what sins God had forgiven and thank Him and suggested where he should read in the Bible.

The next day he looked troubled.

"Something strange happened last night. I took my Bible out

from under the bed. It just fell open to: Ezekiel 36:24-28

For I will take you from among the heathen, and gather you out of all countries, and will bring you into your own land. Then will I sprinkle clean water upon you, and ye shall be clean: from all your filthiness, and from all your idols, will I cleanse you. A new heart also will I give you, and a new spirit will I put within you: and I will take away the stony heart out of your flesh, and I will give you a heart of flesh. And I will put my spirit within you, and cause you to walk in my statutes, and ye shall keep my judgments, and do them. And ye shall dwell in the land that I gave to your fathers; and ye shall be my people, and I will be your God.

"That was God, wasn't it?"

Stunned, I nodded yes, as I had asked God if he was telling the truth.

"I was sitting on my bed mesmerized, man! Then the Bible fell open again and these words seem to light up and stand out:

Acts 12:7, 8 And, behold, the angel of the Lord came upon him, and a light shined in the prison: and he smote Peter on the side, and raised him up, saying, Arise up quickly. And his chains fell off from his hands. And the angel said unto him, Gird thyself, and bind on thy sandals. And so he did. And he said unto him, Cast thy garment about thee, and follow me."

I assured him, "It really is God talking to you. You're going to lead young people to Jesus. Instead of leading them into drugs and trouble as before, you're going to change lives for God."

I soon heard him preaching stories in the Bible in jive talk. "This cat Elizabeth was Mary's homie…"

He brought his best friend Earl to me and after many talks with him, Earl also gave his life to Jesus. Then they later got mad at each other. I brought them together.

"You're letting the devil get between you. Think about it: You both came from the same neighborhood…You're homies. You both

CHAPTER 17

committed different crimes, were arrested, sentenced to the same
prison, the same quad, the same building, and got saved within
three weeks of each other. God's got a plan to use both of you!
Now make up." They hugged and were friends again.

And months later Earl sadly told me his wife was dying from
cancer. God told me to tell him she was going to be healed of cancer.
I tested the spirit, made sure it *was* God and then told him. Awhile
later he described how his wife went to a church service, a visiting
evangelist prayed for her, and Jesus healed her of cancer!

God Uses My Dusty Shoes

And it's wonderful how God gets me where he wants me. God
heard Hector crying out to Him three nights in a row and sent me
to him. I had been planning to have my shoes shined after work
before leaving the institution but forgot until I reached my car. So
I decided to go to the shoeshine man outside instead of returning
inside the prison. It cost the same amount of script.

The shoeshine man had left, however, so the inmate barber,
Hector, said he could do it. I started talking about the Lord while
Hector shined my shoes, and he excitedly told me he had been
asking God for help for three nights. Jesus ended up saving and
then baptizing him in the Holy Spirit. He just glowed and shivered
from the power of God on him, PTL!

Grace for John

Another time, I found extra pants in John's locker and called
him into the office. He barely started talking and I interrupted him
with, "You're a con man manipulator, and I don't even want to
talk to you." He started to say something, and I again interrupted
him saying the same thing. When he protested that he hadn't even
talked yet and how could I know anything about him, I told him ,
"God showed me you're a manipulator."

Then I added, "You were a cute little boy and was spoiled and got away with a lot. And then you grew up and flattered and manipulated women."

He was surprised, asking, "God told you that?" Then he told me he had a terrible dream the night before. He hadn't told anyone because it was so terrible. He dreamed that he tried to make love to his sister.

I blurted out, "That's sick!" and he agreed.

I explained that when he rebelled and sinned against God, that opened the door for demons to take control over areas of his life. And now demons were planting seeds and wanted him to start imagining and fantasizing, so he would parole and end up raping her.

And then he told me that a few weeks earlier he was tired of being the way he was and wanted to change and went to the chapel. He saw an inmate with tattoos on his face testifying. He could see in that inmate's face and eyes that God had changed him, and John wanted that, too. He stood up when they gave the altar call. When he saw no one else had stood up and everyone was staring at him, he got mad.

"There were about 200 guys in there and none of them stood up, just me. Why did they go there if they didn't want God to change them? They put their hands on me and prayed for me but nothing happened."

I explained, "Most of them had already answered an altar call at some time and were saved. I know you were sincere then, and Satan stole that moment from you by having you distracted thinking about the other men. But God knows your heart and is giving you another chance."

Tears came to his eyes. He didn't understand salvation so I explained. I stressed surrendering and commitment from the heart not the head, being willing to repent and turn around and go the other direction, and not fearing what others thought. He was ready, and Jesus saved and baptized him in the Holy Spirit. He really felt Jesus come in and knew He's real.

Russian Roulette

Paul came to my dorm to do some plumbing work. He told me he was a back-slid Christian. He told me he experienced terrible child abuse but had succeeded in his own plumbing business until he injured himself and couldn't work. He lost everything and his wife left him. Every day at a motel, for two weeks he loaded four rounds into the six chambers of his pistol and put it to his temple and pulled the trigger. Each time he said, "Well, guess God doesn't want me to die," and then went to work.

He would phone his parents and just say, "I love you and am thinking about you," and then hang up. Finally his parents went to the motel. He said, "Look, I can't kill myself," and put the gun to his temple and pulled the trigger several times after spinning it each time. He did the same several times in front of a friend, too, another time.

I exclaimed, "God supernaturally kept you from killing yourself to keep you from going to hell!"

I counseled him about total commitment and forgiveness, etc.; and although it was difficult for him, he finally prayed with me asking God to help him forgive all those who had hurt him. He felt deliverance and joy and peace and then gave his life back to Jesus. And after I explained, Jesus baptized him in the Holy Spirit with the evidence of praying in tongues.

Better than Gold Teeth

Soon I met Charles, a very joyous Black with two front teeth missing. He had been a very angry man until he got saved three months earlier. Before, when anyone teased him about his missing teeth, he would beat them up. Now he just laughs and tells them he has more joy without his teeth than they would be if all their teeth were gold. He didn't know about the BHS until I explained. When I prayed for him to receive, he felt overwhelmed as God came down as consuming fire. He felt burning hot and prayed so joyfully and loudly in tongues, I had to quiet him so I wouldn't get into trouble.

Buddhist Transformed

One day an older Asian man, Luke, came rushing into the dorm. He was greatly agitated and said he needed help and heard that I helped inmates. He explained that he was supposed to parole today but they delayed it three weeks. I told him God wanted to use this extra time to bring him to Jesus so He could change his life and keep him from returning. "Oh, you're a Christian," he sneered. "I'm a Buddhist." As we talked, he admitted praying to Buddha hadn't helped him.

He asked me to pray for God to change his wife's mind and let him see his sons. Instead I was led to pray for God to make Himself real to him so he could surrender, get delivered from alcoholism, for the wife to see the change in him, and then let him see his sons.

Two days later, Luke stopped me in the yard to say he slept peacefully for 12 hours the day we prayed. He was astounded because usually he's too anxious to sleep hardly at all. Then the next two days he couldn't stop thinking about God. So went to my dorm office, and I explained the gospel. He asked lots of questions, "counting the cost" of salvation. He showed me the picture of Buddha that his mom gave him. "I always carry this around. If I become a Christian, I can't carry this around anymore?"

I explained, "With Jesus in your heart, you'll be so happy, you won't need it anymore because Jesus is alive and Buddha is dead."

Jesus gloriously saved him. He was so happy and thrilled.

"I've never felt anything like this before." Without any prompting, he took out the picture of Buddha. "Even though my mom gave this to me, I'm throwing this in the toilet." And he tore it in pieces, crossed the hall, and flushed it down!

As I was explaining the BHS, he said, "I don't want this. I think I should take things slowly." I explained, "Remember I told you the carnal mind is an enemy against God and will always argue against the things of God. The devil doesn't want your carnal mind to lose control, because that's where he puts thoughts in your mind that will cause you to fall." So he changed his mind and desired all that God had for him and received his prayer language and was even happier.

Luke came in the next three days and I taught him for about 30 minutes each time to reinforce his resolve not to ever fall away from Jesus. He had been concerned he might have to serve more time in another state before being released. But the day before he left, he said, "I told God last night: If you want me to stay in prison longer instead of paroling, it's because I'm not strong enough to stay out. You love me and know best. So I understand that if I don't parole it's because I'm not ready. I trust You."

What a change in attitude! I asked him to promise to tell a group of five Asians, who congregate daily to play cards, that he gave his life to Jesus. "I don't want to lose this peace and joy. I know they'll ridicule me and will say mean things. So I won't tell them until the morning that I parole." And he did. And they _did_ laugh.

Migraines Healed

Rick was one of the Asians that laughed at Luke. I heard he had terrible migraine headaches every day. One day I asked him how his headache was. He said it was so bad he skipped lunch. Then he asked what caused them. I told him there's an unseen dimension where there are demons and angels. And that the headaches were demonic sent by the devil because he hates us all. I told him the gospel then said, "I know you aren't ready to give your life to Jesus now. But I could pray for you and ask God to help you want to give your life to Him." He agreed. When I prayed, I felt led to put one finger on his forehead and rebuke the headaches in Jesus' name. Jesus delivered him of that throbbing headache instantly. In wonderment, he exclaimed, "The pain left! I feel so good! How do I give my life to God?" He followed me in prayer and felt Jesus come in and take the weight of sin off. I explained the BHS, and he received. The migraine headaches never returned.

Wind On the Range

And of course God doesn't always make it easy and comfortable for us. While one Christian officer always prayed for and received beautiful weather when it was time to qualify at the range, it would sometimes be very windy weather for me. I was wondering if my faith wasn't as strong as his. Then God explained He was increasing my faith by showing me He helped me score high even when the wind was blowing me around. I didn't have to have ideal conditions to do well. And working early or late hours at night in the cold outdoors toughened me instead of pampering me.

Screams Near A Gun Tower

One day at the range I noticed a woman officer was nervous and afraid she wouldn't qualify.

I asked, "Do you believe in prayer?"

"Oh yes."

"Would you like me to pray for you?"

"Please do!"

"Dear Lord, please have Your peace and calm fall on her. Help her to cast this care on You. Help her to trust You and help her to qualify and we'll give You the praise. In Jesus' Name we pray. Amen."

After she qualified I asked, "Would you like to learn about the Baptism of the Holy Spirit?"

So we drove our two cars to an empty space in back of a gun tower. She got in mine. I explained about the Baptism of the Holy Spirit. When I started to pray for her to receive, she started screaming very loudly!

I thought, "Ohmygosh, here we are in our civies behind a gun tower and this woman is screaming bloody murder!"

Then I realized God was in control, that He must be delivering her, and rebuked the devil, she got set free, received her prayer language, and was thrilled and overjoyed.

Rest Instead of Religion

I was in a dorm office when another Paul entered. "I heard you help inmates. I pray for four hours every day and read the Bible two hours every day. But there's no fruit. I've never led anyone to Jesus. What's wrong?"

While he was talking, I sent a quick prayer up to God.

"Is he telling the truth? I don't pray or read that much. He should pray for me!" God showed me he was telling the truth and had me say,

"God is so pleased with your devotion and discipline and desire to please Him. But a religious spirit sneaked in, and now you're doing it as a routine."

I explained Hebrews chapters 3 and 4 and explained the difference between "works of the flesh" and entering into His rest and how anything done in the flesh comes to nothing. Then I told him God was going to deliver him from the religious spirit and prayed with one finger touching his shoulder. He felt the power of God go through him and left happy.

I went to another assignment and returned three weeks later. Paul told me he had led two people to salvation during that interim!

Then he stood in the yard and watched inmates returning from lunch. God would show him who to approach. In a prison it's not wise to go up to strangers unless God is leading you. He would say, "God shows me you're a Christian. Would you like to know about the fullness of God in a new dimension?" When they said yes, Paul would ask me if he could bring that person to me that day.

"Stay and take notes, Paul, while I explain the Baptism of the Holy Spirit and pray for him."

Seven inmates received their prayer language over a few weeks. When Paul wanted to bring the eighth man, God told me to tell him,

"God wants you to lead this man into the Baptism of the Holy Spirit, Paul."

"Oh no. I might not do it right. I don't want to hurt anyone's faith by their not receiving."

"Paul, you know how and you hear God. I'll pray for God's anointing to fall on you to empower you."

This time when I prayed for him, Paul said,

"Before I felt God's power shoot through me. This time the power went through me but stopped at my finger tips. I know I can now."

And soon Paul had led three men to receive the Baptism of the Holy Spirit.

Faith and Finances

Paul always kept an accurate account of how much money he had in his account. He was sitting in the prison chapel and knew the amount to withdraw for offering when God told him to give a larger amount. He argued with God.

"If I give that amount, there won't be enough money in my account to pay for the chicken dinner I've already reserved."

From time to time inmate groups are allowed to raise money by selling Kentucky Fried Chicken.

But God was not to be dissuaded. Paul was jittery as he wrote down the amount God said on his withdrawal slip. You can imagine his relief when he learned the chicken dinner was postponed to a later date. God was stretching his faith.

My Definition of Faith

Faith is hearing God and obeying. And it doesn't matter if you're trembling with fear when you obey. It takes more courage to obey when you are afraid, and that's exhibiting real faith.

Over Powered in the Yard

David was another remarkable inmate. His love for Jesus was apparent when I first met him in the dorm for newcomers. I helped him to receive the Baptism of the Holy Spirit, and he was even more exuberant.

He confided in me that he was sad because he didn't know how to read well, and he knew how important it is to read the Bible. I told him about three people I knew who God supernaturally taught to read. We prayed and I asked God to teach him to read then told him as he made an effort, God would start teaching him. And not much later, God was doing exactly that.

As he matured, he started teaching in the yard. God had him call over two white guys he didn't know. Normally a black inmate wouldn't do that. He obeyed and when they came over, as he prayed for one, the man fell to the ground under the power of God.

"Oh no! The tower officer will think I stabbed him and will shoot me!" he thought terrified.

"Who do you think put him under the power? I'm in control. Pray for the other man," was God's command.

David obeyed, and the other man also fell to the ground.

Now David is off parole and is a pastor and feeds the homeless.

God Cares About Toothpaste

Bob learned you can't out give God. He felt inside that he was to give his toothpaste away to a new inmate he had been telling about God. But Bob didn't want to. The tube was over half full. He wouldn't be eligible to go to canteen for two more weeks, and he hated the taste of the free prison tooth powder. Reluctantly he gave his toothpaste away. And that same day, Bob found someone had put a brand new tube of his favorite toothpaste under his cell door!

Shining Light

Another day, a Mexican named Angel came up to me saying he was a Christian and wanted to ask me about healing. The prison doctors performed surgery on him and caused nerve damage, which resulted in his muscles relaxing causing his knee to pop out. They wanted to operate on him, but he was trusting God to heal him. It really touched my heart when he told me his cell partner asked why he kneels to pray when it causes him so much pain. He said, "Jesus suffered so much for me, how could I not kneel to pray to my Lord and Savior." His spontaneous expression of love brought tears to my eyes.

After I explained about the BHS and he prayed in tongues, he just glowed. I knew from the Lord that it was a holy moment and not to interrupt. I could tell something supernatural was happening. He couldn't talk for awhile. Finally told me, in awe, he felt a hand reach inside and take something out. He received deliverance. And he said he thought he was a tiny little light; but God showed him he had a huge shining Light inside of him; and that Light is Jesus who is burning out the darkness.

Miracle Received In A Gun Tower

One time I was temporarily assigned to a gun tower overseeing a sally port. I talked to an officer in another tower. He told me his knee was hurting, and he was dreading having another surgery. As I prayed for him to receive the BHS, he received his prayer language; and God healed his knee instantly at the same time! When his shift was over before mine, he was below in the sally port. Suddenly he started happily dancing a jig below me to show me he was healed!!!

Just then the phone rang for a conference call with all the towers. I was laughing when they took the roll call. The Watch Commander phoned me to ask why I was laughing – to share the joke. I prayed and felt God said, "It's OK. Tell how Jesus healed the officer, and he was dancing." After I told him there was a moment of stunned silence, then he sputtered, "Keep up the good work." A few years later I had more opportunities to share with that lieutenant, and he's now a Christian.

Joy and Fulfillment

These are just a few examples. God showed me that every job change was for a specific purpose and to reach certain individuals. I ended up enjoying the Vacation-Relief assignments I once feared and dreaded. Over the years, I worked *all* the assignments on both East and West Facilities except the very few jobs women couldn't work. I even worked some of those positions all three watches. Even though I still was apprehensive at times, the joy and fulfillment outweighed any negatives.

And although other officers and supervisors didn't know the extent of my activities, my actions did not go unnoticed.

CHAPTER 18

Criticized and Chastised

Many of the staff were referring to me as the Bible Thumping Jesus Freak or Convict Lover and were scornful of me.

I was aware some inmates like to take advantage of every opportunity to break rules or even do dangerous, evil deeds. So I would interrupt my sharing sessions by taking security checks in the buildings or dorms. And while praying with inmates or staff, I learned to touch God while praying with my eyes open and looking around. I knew I was often more alert while praying than some staff were while they were talking to each other and not looking around or being attentive.

But as I said before, many unbelievers think Christians are ignorant, gullible, and too trusting.

There are 6" keys to lock the front doors of the housing units and the lock box to the lever that unlocks the doors to one side of a cell block wing. These two keys used to remain with the building officer on the midnight watch. After years, for security purposes, those keys were taken away at night and returned in the morning.

Chapter 18

The rumor went around the whole institution for years that those keys were taken away because Honey used to open cell doors to go inside the cell to pray with inmates in the middle of the night! And if that story didn't make me appear foolish enough, there was another tale circulating: Honey used to open several cells so inmates could have a prayer meeting with her in the middle of the night.

I was shocked how many Christians believed those fanciful tales and also spread the rumor. And no one would tell me who told them. I protested that if I was dumb enough to do that I would get raped, killed, or at least fired from the job. And God gives me wisdom not stupidity.

Finally after years, I traced it to a religious officer who was not born again. I told him I knew he started that rumor. He told me a certain sergeant told him.

I phoned that man. "Sergeant, you know I was always alert and diligent in my duties. Tell that officer that story isn't true."
He gave a guilty laugh and promised he would. Within a few minutes the contrite officer called and humbly apologized. I told him,
"Imagine standing on a windy street corner and releasing a big bag of feathers and watching them get blown away by the wind. Just as impossible it would be to gather those feathers back, that's how impossible it is to retrieve all the rumors and damage that story caused me. But I forgive you."

I suppose probably the sergeant had jokingly said after administration decided to take the keys away,

"Well, now we don't have to worry about Honey going into cells….."

And then that joke turned into the rumor that many believed as fact.

Sexual Harassment By A Lieutenant

One morning I went to the Watch Office to check in. The Watch Lieutenant in front of one or two sergeants, officers, and inmates said,

"Well Moy, how's your sex life?"

Moy was my former husband's last name, and this was before sexual harassment laws were in effect. If it happened later, I could have sued him and won a million dollars, as two women did, plus they would have taken away his lieutenant bars.

"Well, lieutenant, at one time I didn't think I could live without sex. But anything we can't control ourselves, if we give it to God, He gives us power over it. Sex is such a beautiful gift from God, He doesn't want it tainted nor tarnished.

"I didn't want to lose my sexuality nor sensuality, but it's as though God put my desires in storage. And when He brings my husband to me, it'll be right and good."

I saw his facial expression turn from mocking scorn, to shock, to shame, and then to hardness as he rejected the Lord.

Afterward, one of the officers said admiringly,

"Wow, that was a good answer. He'll never dare tease *you* again!"

Salvation in the Metal Detector Booth

Another day I was processing men through a metal detector in a little building about 7' x 7'. The room had an open door on both sides and a window on the wall opposite from where I was standing.

An inmate I had talked to about God before came to the doorway and said,

"I've been reading the Bible and praying."

"That's really good," I said approvingly.

Suddenly the next thing I knew, he was kneeling on the other side of the counter, sobbing,

"I need for Jesus to save me. I need Jesus to change me. Right now!"

Usually I take the inmate aside to talk to him. But this man was kneeling and wailing loudly. So I put a finger on his shoulder and led him in repeating a prayer after me.

"Jesus, I believe You are the Son of God. I believe You died for me and You rose from the dead so I can have eternal life. I've done things I'm ashamed of and need You to forgive me and wash my heart clean. Please come into my heart and forgive me. I surrender my life to You.

"Thank You for coming in. Thank You for forgiving me. Thank You for washing my heart clean. I'm Yours. Teach me how to love You and follow You."

By now he was sobbing even more, but this time with joy.

But at the start of the prayer, I saw an officer's shocked face looking in the door.

"I'm in trouble now," I thought as I continued the prayer.

Sure enough he had told a sergeant who also looked in the door. As the sergeant was hurrying away to report me to the Watch Office, I saw him repeatedly look back through the open door viewing us both still praying.

Soon an officer came to relieve me at this post and told me to report to the Watch Office.

The Sergeant and Watch Sergeant lectured me and gave me a disciplinary report. I made certain they added an important fact they omitted: There was a counter between me and the kneeling inmate.

Submission to Authority

Another time an inmate told a sergeant I was praying for inmates, so I was lectured and written up again.

Although I believe in being submissive to authority, I knew leading inmates and staff to Jesus was the purpose for my being there. And I knew I was doing my job well and not neglecting duties and always was alert when I prayed with my eyes open. So since I believe God's authority is higher than prison authority, I continued as opportunities presented themselves.

When staff realized I wasn't going to stop, they seemed to avoid wherever I worked. If they didn't see me, they didn't have to report me.

And I'm well aware there are many violent, dangerous inmates who consider staff their enemy, especially at several other institutions. Inmates have thrown collected feces and urine at officers' faces. I commend the courageous staff working under such daily hazardous conditions where their lives are in jeopardy.

I'm so grateful I worked at this particular institution where perilous incidents are less common. When criticized, I explained my stance is that I want to help the men change before they leave the prison and become my neighbors. Several staffers' attitudes toward me changed when they recognized the validity of that ideology.

And during my latter years, there were supportive Christian Associate Wardens, Captains, Lieutenants, Program Administrators, and Sergeants who knew what I was doing and encouraged me.

Meanwhile God was using me away from the prison as well.

Divine Assignments Away from the Prison

Quite often I asked the Lord to have my path cross someone I could lead to Jesus that day or bless in some other way. And that request has led to many more fun adventures.

After ministering in meetings in San Diego and Anaheim, while returning on Amtrak, I saw a tall, thin satanic-looking man with black fingernail polish, black eyeliner, long dyed black hair, black clothing, body and numerous face piercings and rings, and nail studded leather wrist bands. As he walked through my rail car, I breathed a prayer, "Lord, I'd like to tell him about You. Please make a way."

Awhile later he took the seat behind me, so I prayed for an opening to talk to him. A short while later, I felt the back of my seat go bump, bump, bump. I peeked around the side and said, "You're so nice and tall, I bet you're terribly uncomfortable cramped up in these tiny seats."

He mumbled, "Man am I hung over." He went on to explain he had just finished a long tour of Europe with a famous rock band as a substitute drummer. He marveled, "I can't believe they chose me. I can't believe I'm back in America on a train. I can't believe I didn't take a drink before I got on."

I changed my seat to sit across the aisle alongside of him. I could smell the stench of alcohol coming from him. As we talked I could see he had a really tender heart. His dad died when he was nine, and some Christians told him, "God needed him and took him home."

He said bitterly, "Either there's no God, or He's a cruel God to take a little boy's dad."

"I don't believe God took him." I continued, "Sometimes God warns people not to do something, but they don't heed the warning."

"And a year later my mom's boyfriend would constantly beat me. I cried out to God, 'God, if You stop him, I'll be a priest. I'll be a minister. Whatever You want I'll do. Just stop him.'" He angrily continued, "God didn't stop him. Either there is no God or He's cruel and just doesn't care." My heart went out to him.

I explained, "Some things we'll never understand this side of eternity. But I do know it hurt God's heart that you were being abused because He's full of love for you. I believe He *did* want someone to stop that man. But because of fear or intimidation or lack of obedience, they didn't intervene. But that's not God's fault, because I believe He wanted them to."

"Maybe I could accept that," he said. Then he went on to tell me how he lives in Hollywood but goes to downtown Los Angeles to try to help African kids 8-12 years old stay out of gangs. He told them, "Sure I hate homework. I hated it when I was your age and I hate doing it now. But I'll sit down with you and help you do your homework if that's what it takes. You have to graduate." And he helped one kid go from F to B. Parents have phoned to thank him.

I told him I knew he wasn't ready to give his life to the Lord yet, but I wanted to explain what salvation meant. He really listened. And I told him what to pray when he was ready later. And when I asked him if I could pray with him to get his heart ready, he agreed. We held hands and I prayed for God's protection over him, for God to put a desire in his heart to know Him, and for him to be able to surrender to God's love one day so God could bless him the way He wants to, and so I could see him in heaven one day.

He felt the presence of God. He told me, "I know you're really sincere and caring. You didn't judge or reject me or turn away. Maybe there is a God." He gave me his email address and also his home address. I was so engrossed in our conversation, I mistakenly got off the train at the stop 40 miles too soon. I had to phone for a ride home. But I was sooooo happy God touched David's heart, it was worth the wait in the cold darkness. (Please, everyone reading this pray for David to give his life to Jesus.)

Special Usher and My Angel Ring

Remember Paul who prayed for people to receive the Baptism of the Holy Spirit? Years later after Paul was off parole, he worked for a large corporation where he supervised a warehouse containing ten million dollars worth of merchandise. I was going to a Christian conference at the Anaheim Convention Center now known as The Pond. Paul was going to be among the 200 ushers. He didn't have a cell phone, but we believed God was going to help us find each other out of the 8,000 people there.

On the way there on a chartered bus, I noticed my favorite ring was loose on my finger, because it was so cold my finger shrunk. If I put it in my purse, it would get scratched. If I wrapped it in tissue, I might forget and toss it away. So I left it on my finger.

When we arrived we were told our usher would meet our group at the top of the stairs. And yes, the usher waiting there was Paul! We hugged and praised the Lord together.

Later when I returned from going to the restroom, I discovered my ring wasn't on my finger. I rushed back, searched through the trash, but didn't find my ring. I sadly put the trash back in the container. I looked under the seat and later under the bus seat, all to no avail.

I remembered how an evangelist told on TV that when she was at an airport, she dropped her jewelry box. Her jewelry scattered. She found all but her favorite ring and asked God to have an angel return it to her. Awhile later her husband found the ring in *his* jewelry box, and neither goes into each other's things.

So I prayed, "You're not a respecter of persons. Please have an angel return my ring as you did for her, and place it where I'll know an angel did it."

Every time I thought about my ring, I praised God that an angel was returning my ring to me. And about two weeks later, I found my ring on my living room floor right where I often walk. God delights in showing His love for us in special ways.

Rejoicing At A Funeral

My friend in Sacramento asked me to conduct and preach at his dad's funeral. The day before the funeral, I was able to lead the widow (who I hadn't met yet) to salvation over the telephone. And Jesus saved at least 21 attendees at the funeral!! (I counted the upraised hands out loud so the family could rejoice.)

And after the service, outside of the funeral parlor, my hostess introduced me to a correctional counselor who had been a sergeant before. God showed me some things to pray with him about, which brought tears to his eyes.

And that opened the way for him to want the baptism of the Holy Spirit. What a loving God we have!!! He received with much sobbing. He almost went under the power and hung onto an unsaved security squad officer standing nearby, who was under conviction and wanted to get away but couldn't and had to listen. This counselor's wife left him five years earlier, and his 14-year-old son was aloof and distant to him. God told me to tell him to humble himself, apologize to the son for the way he used to be, and to tell the boy that he's sorry, and that God is changing him. In the spirit, I could see him and his son both crying and hugging, and God restoring their relationship. He hugged and thanked me, still crying.

Rabbi's Son

While traveling to Israel in July 2000, I met a handsome Israeli man at the Newark, New Jersey airport. I knew to quietly listen for over 45 minutes as he told me about himself. He was the 13th of 14 children born to a Rabbi. He didn't tell me, but God showed me his dad was a harsh disciplinarian and very authoritative.

So I told him of Father God's love and how He had a plan for each life. He allowed me to pray with him at the airport. I asked God to draw him with His love so he could surrender some day, so God could bless his life abundantly. I had my hand on his arm, and he put his hand on top of my arm as I prayed. When I finished, he said, "My heart is pounding!"

I exclaimed, "That's Yeshua knocking on the door of your heart!"

He said, "Maybe I should let him in?" -- ! (Without my telling him that, he knew!) But then he counted the cost and didn't at that time.

We've emailed since then sporadically. He travels to different countries as a computer engineer, went to serve in the Israeli military at least twice since then, received a promotion on the job but still travels, was on the third floor at work when the earthquake hit near Tel Aviv, and all the occupants ran out the building.

Soon after, I felt it was God's timing for him. So in an email,

I wrote to him about his being surrounded by danger, explained the gospel again with scriptures and what it meant to walk with Yeshua and be under His protection, etc., and wrote out a prayer for him to pray if he was ready. And he wrote back telling how he prayed that prayer and felt God's presence as he did when I prayed with him at the NJ airport!

Miracle In Doctor's Waiting Room

While sitting in the doctor's waiting room, a woman who looked and sounded like she came from a rough background came in connected to an oxygen tank. She started talking about the weather to the man between us. I joined their conversation. She said something about the future being scary. I told her for me: knowing the Lord made all the difference in the world. She lighted up, and I told briefly about working at the prison and the difference knowing Jesus made. She said she got saved three months ago.

Her vision was bad as she had cataracts. I told her about my friend getting healed watching Benny Hinn on TV and wrote the information about his program down for her. The man between us asked me to repeat the information. She said she was afraid of losing her vision. I told her about some of the ones I prayed for who received healing.

There were four others in the waiting room so I didn't want to, but I felt God wanted me to ask if she wanted me to pray for her. She said an enthusiastic YES. So I had to ignore what the others might be thinking. I also had to ignore the thoughts bombarding my mind, "What if she's not healed? That will reinforce their thinking Christians are kooky!"

I sat next to her and prayed for her vision and her lungs to be healed. I explained sometimes the healings are instantaneous and sometimes it's progressive. I told her to take off her glasses and look across the room at the picture. She said she could see it more clearly than before. I told her to close her eyes and expect to see it more clearly and open and look again. She was getting excited as her vision was still more clear. I had her do it a few times. She described that she could see details that she couldn't before. I sat back across the room, and she could see my face clearly!!! I explained how to keep her healing. I told her to expect her lungs to get better but to not do anything foolish. She was so happy!

Thank you, Jesus. He's such a sweet, loving, wonderful God!!!

Hardest Test for Me

Now I'll relate one of the hardest things God ever had me do. At a home meeting while we were praying for a woman, I felt God wanted me to punch this slim, frail 70-year-old woman hard in the stomach! I knew it was for deliverance. I kept praying to make sure it was God. If it wasn't Him, she could go to the hospital injured, and I could go to jail! I told the leader of the group, and she said hesitantly, "Well….If you feel it's God, go ahead and do it."

I asked her to please stand up. She had her eyes closed and was praying, standing there so trusting with her hands by her sides and her face upturned to God. I explained about healing and then said, "Not by power, not by might, but by Your Holy Spirit," had my arm back and my fist poised, but I couldn't make myself hit her. We prayed some more and I repeated the scripture, but again couldn't hit her.

And I wanted to tell her to tighten her stomach, so it wouldn't hurt as much, but felt God didn't want me to. I prayed, "God if you want me to, You're going to have to help me." Finally I hit her with my fist in the stomach. She groaned, "Umph," and fell backwards onto the couch. I knew it was for deliverance so expected a smile. Instead she gave me an angry look.

I asked God, "That *was* You, wasn't it?" I felt He said, "Yes," so started praising Him in spite of everything. The leader then was comforting her with her arms around her, which didn't make me feel any better. The others looked at me as though I was weird.

Later that evening, I told the woman, "You know I didn't want to do that, and it was nothing personal, don't you?"

She answered, "Oh yes, I knew it was God. Actually it felt rather good." Why didn't she tell me that before the others left! And still later that evening, she thanked me for my obedience. She said when she first arrived, she had shooting pains in her side and stomach. But after God had me punch her, the shooting pains disappeared, and now she felt fine. Whew. Thank you, Jesus!

After I punched the woman, the leader told how Smith Wigglesworth drop kicked an *infant* into the air!!! The Mom ran to catch the baby! And the baby was healed of cancer! What an awesome God. Of course God had trained Smith well by then, so he was able to have the faith to do that.

I guess that's how we grow: Inch by inch.

My Prayer

One day I was feeling lonely. I'm so glad I don't feel lonely very often; but that day I did. I told the Lord I missed loving a man and being loved in return. I asked the Lord, "Does Your heart ever get lonely?"

He surprised me with His answer, "Yes, I do. I love multitudes. But the multitude is made up of individuals, and I receive love back from relatively few out of that multitude. And My heart has lonely spots when those individuals don't love Me back. Each spot can only be filled with the love that particular individual can give."

My heart ached, and it was as if I felt the Lord's pain. I cried and cried and prayed in tongues for over an hour. Then I said, "I want to love You more. Fill me more and send me to even more who don't know You and Your love. I want to tell them about You and Your love so they will surrender and love You back and fill up those empty spots in Your heart!"

I hope this book will encourage you to be a light and a witness wherever you are: At home, with your relatives and friends, at school, at work, with strangers. Ask Holy Spirit to give you boldness.   And ask God to give you divine appointments, too. There are so many hurting people who will be receptive to hearing how Jesus can change their lives. Seeing lives transformed is worth any ridicule or persecution that might come your way.

Be like a garden hose. You must be attached to the correct faucet (Holy Spirit), fairly free of impediments and hindrances inside, have the faucet turned on, and have the water (Holy Spirit anointed words and His love) flowing freely through you aimed at the right target.

Don't have Him ride piggy back while you're trying to do it *for* Him. Remember to let *Him* do it *through* you. You be the glove, and allow Him to be the hand inside moving the glove.

May you have the joy that comes from divine appointments!

The Phenomenon of Tongues

W hat is "tongues?? Why did God give it? What is its purpose? Can all Christians pray in tongues? I'll attempt to answer these questions.

Helps Us Express Ourselves Through A Love Connection

Sometimes it's hard to pray very long in our natural language. We just run out of words. And sometimes when we're hurting really badly, we can't even begin to express to God what we're feeling inside. And other times when we're really happy, we can't really thank God the way we want to. We just don't have the words to express our appreciation.

Well, God, in His wisdom, has this beautiful gift for us to express our innermost thoughts and feelings through the Holy Spirit within us being released through us. It's a divine stream flowing from our heart to God's heart and back and forth. It's a *DIVINE LOVE CONNECTION*.

And it was predicted in the Old Testament. Zephaniah 3:9 says: "For then will I turn to the people a pure language that they may all call upon the name of the Lord, to serve Him with one consent." We know every earthly language has curses and obscenities. The only language that is pure is a heavenly prayer language: tongues.

And in James 3 we read how our tongue is evil and hard to control. That's another reason why God wants us to surrender our tongues so the Lord can pray through us.

Jesus Desires the Baptism and Tongues For Us

It is <u>so</u> important to God, it was the last thing Jesus talked to his disciples about just before He left for heaven. Jesus said in Mark 16:17: "And these signs shall follow them that believe: In my Name shall they cast out devils; they shall speak with new tongues."

To further show its importance, Acts 1:4 and 5: "And, being assembled together with them, (Jesus) commanded them that they should not depart from Jerusalem but "wait for the promise of the Father, which," saith He, "Ye have heard of me. For John truly baptized with water, but ye shall be baptized with the Holy Ghost not many days hence."

After we've accepted Jesus as Saviour, we have the Holy Spirit in us. And if we died, we'd go to heaven. But He wants to come <u>upon</u> us. For instance: When we take a drink of water, we have some water inside us. However, when we dive into a lake, we're immersed and surrounded by water. So it is with the Baptism of the Holy Spirit.

Gives Us Power

And Acts 1:8 says: But ye shall receive power after that the Holy Ghost is come upon you; and ye shall be witnesses unto me both in Jerusalem, and in all Judaea and in Samaria, and unto the uttermost part of the earth."

The three places symbolize the place where we live, our neighborhood or city, and wherever God sends us. We surely do need His power to come upon us to be Godly Christians. We surely can't be a good witness by ourselves or be an example that would cause others to think about becoming a Christian themselves without the Holy Spirit helping us. We need His love and compassion and power to flow through us.

Gives us Faith

Jude verse 20 says: "But ye, beloved, building up yourselves on your most holy faith, praying in the Holy Ghost."

When we're praying in tongues, we're surrendering our wicked tongues, and we're opening our hearts up to God like a funnel, so He can pour His faith into our hearts so we can believe Him for the miracles He longs to do in our lives.

Makes Us Strong Inside

After we're saved, we have a new nature. But we also still have the old nature, which will always be at war with the new man. Whichever nature we feed will grow stronger. And whichever we starve will get weaker. So just as we exercise to make our muscles stronger, we have to exercise our will to say "yes" to God and "no" to Satan and our flesh.

1 Cor. 14:4 says: "He that speaks in an unknown tongue edifieth himself..." An edifice is a building; so we're building up our inner man making him strong against our flesh and the devil when we're praying in tongues.

God's Secret Code

And it's God's Secret Code. In the military they don't pick up a radio and say, "Platoon B meet Platoon A on the west side of the bridge." They know the enemy would intercept the message and blow up the bridge or capture the men. So they speak in a scrambled secret code. And we are certainly in a war with Satan, the enemy of our souls, who is always trying to destroy our souls by making us fall away from Jesus.

The devil can put thoughts into our minds and he can hear our prayers. When we're praying in tongues, Satan can't understand what we're saying. And even though he might know who or what circumstances we're praying for, he doesn't know what God's strategy is. So he can't put up hindrances to block the prayer from being answered as he did in Daniel 10:12 and 13.

It's the Best Way to Pray Because We're Praying God's Will

When we pray in our own language we often are praying incorrectly because, although we can see the problem or circumstances, we don't know the root problem or what caused the circumstances.

Apostle Paul said in Romans 8:26 and 27: "Likewise the Spirit also helps our infirmities (our weaknesses and inadequacies): for we know not what we should pray for as we ought: but the Spirit itself makes intercession for us with groanings which cannot be uttered.

"And He that searcheth the hearts knows what is the mind of the Spirit because He makes intercession for the saints according to the will of God."

That's really exciting! Even though God is all powerful and can do anything He wants, He gives us the privilege and joy of releasing much of His power on earth through our faith and prayers. When we're praying in tongues, we're praying His perfect will for the situation. And we're breaking demonic strongholds over people and situations.

Breaking Demonic Powers

There's an unseen dimension where there are angels and demons. God gives some individuals the gift of discerning of spirits so they can actually see the angels and demons from time to time when He wants them to. "For we wrestle not against flesh and blood, but against principalities, against powers, against the rulers of the darkness of this world, against spiritual wickedness in high places." Ephesians 6:12.

When we're thinking of someone or a situation and releasing our faith and prayer language, we're actually breaking the power of darkness over them in the spirit world so we can have the victory in this physical world. Sometimes I actually feel as though I'm punching demons' lights out when I'm interceding and/or rebuking in tongues!

For instance: When I was new Christian only about one month saved, I knew a close friend who I will call Rita was deeply depressed but I didn't know why. She hadn't confided in me, and I didn't want to pry. When I started praying for her, instead of sounding light and happy, I sounded like I was scolding in tongues. This startled me as I hadn't been taught and this had never occurred before. I stopped for a moment, since we always have control. I tried to make my voice sound cheerful, but the tones still came out sounding angry. This went on for a few minutes, then my tones sounded normal again. And my tones sounded normal for everyone else I prayed for that day. This continued for about two weeks. I only sounded like I was scolding when I prayed for Rita.

Then for one week, Thursday through Wednesday, my tongues sounded cheerful for Rita as for everyone else. Then exactly after one week, I started scolding in tongues again when I prayed for Rita. After two or three weeks, I told Rita what was happening. She asked me when this happened. I gave her a slip of paper with the dates written down. She took the paper to a calendar. When she returned she confided for the first time that her nice respectable, distinguished-looking professional husband was an alcoholic. He waited every night until the children were in bed before he started drinking. Then he drank and drank until he was very abusive verbally and emotionally to Rita every night.

I didn't know this, but the Holy Spirit did. Every night that he drank and I prayed, the Holy Spirit was rebuking the powers of darkness over this man. Then one week he took his kids on a camping trip with him. They stayed all night with him in the same tent, so he didn't drink the whole week. I didn't know this, but the Holy Spirit did. The whole week that he didn't drink, I didn't rebuke once in tongues. Then when they returned home and he started drinking again, the Holy Spirit in me started rebuking again through me.

Rita asked me what this meant. I asked the Lord and told her, "This is God's way of letting you know He knows your situation. He wants to give you faith to believe. In Matthew 18:18 Jesus said, "Verily I say unto you, Whatsoever ye shall bind on earth shall be bound in heaven; and whatsoever ye shall loose on earth shall be loosed in heaven." We can bind a person or a problem on earth if we worry or are fearful, because that is the opposite of faith, and we're binding God's power from being released from heaven. Instead we should release the person or situation on earth with trust and faith despite what is happening saying, "I don't care what it looks like. I trust you, Jesus. I release him to you and thank you because you _are_ moving mightily in this situation." Then God's power can be released unhindered from heaven.

Power Over Our Carnal Mind

We are a three-part being consisting of spirit, soul, and body with a mind in each area. In 1 Thess. 5:23, Paul says, "And the very God of peace sanctify you wholly; and I pray God your whole spirit and soul and body be preserved blameless unto the coming of our Lord Jesus Christ." Our flesh body is like a tent that will be disposed of when we die. Our soul is the real us, our heart: consisting of our personality, our emotion, our character, our will. God breathed His breath of life into our spirit when we were conceived. After we knowingly sinned, we grieved the Holy Spirit and He left our spirit. Then it's just a human spirit until we ask Jesus to be our Saviour; then when we do, His Holy Spirit infuses our human spirit and lives within us again.

Romans 8:6 and 7: "For to be carnally (flesh) minded is death; but to be spiritually minded is life and peace. Because the carnal mind is enmity (an enemy) against God; for it is not subject to the law of God, neither indeed can be." Our flesh mind in our head will try to take us to hell until the day we die. Our mind in our born-again spirit always wants to do God's will. Our mind in our soul or heart is undecided until it gets converted by the Word of God (Psalm 19:7). It's flaky.

Both the flesh and the spirit are pulling the soul, and whichever way the soul or heart votes that moment is the way we go. But as we pray in tongues, the soul mind gets stronger while the fleshly carnal mind starts losing its control over us. Just as we exercise our muscles to get strong, we have to exercise our will to go God's way not ours. And the more we resist the flesh and the devil, the easier it gets to choose God's way.

When Adam and Eve walked and talked in the Garden of Eden with God, their spirit, soul, and flesh were in unity. Their soul would always listen to their spirit mind, which always communed with the Holy Spirit; so they knew what God wanted them to think. The soul would tell their brain, "Don't think that, think this," and it would obey. After the fall, the flesh mind became the boss: a cruel tyrant. How many times you've wanted to sleep, but the mind is going on and on; you want it to shut up so you can sleep. After we're saved, God wants our soul mind to be the boss again so we can make our flesh mind be a tool instead of the tyrant boss so we can think what God wants us to think. The more we pray in tongues, the more sensitive we become to the Holy Spirit, and the more Spirit led we become.

———

Standing In Adversity

Numbers 23:19 (KJS) God [is] not a man, that he should lie; neither the son of man, that he should repent: hath he said, and shall he not do [it]? or hath he spoken, and shall he not make it good?

Roma 4:20 (KJS) He staggered not at the promise of God through unbelief; but was strong in faith, giving glory to God; 21 And being fully persuaded that, what he had promised, he was able also to perform. 22 And therefore it was imputed to him for righteousness.

2 Cor 4:18 (KJS) While we look not at the things which are seen, but at the things which are not seen: for the things which are seen [are] temporal; but the things which are not seen [are] eternal.

Mark 10:27 (KJS) And Jesus looking upon them saith, With men [it is] impossible, but not with God: for with God all things are possible.

Luke 1:37 (KJS) For with God nothing shall be impossible. 38 And Mary said, Behold the handmaid of the Lord; be it unto me according to thy word. And the angel departed from her.

Interpretation

You can pray in tongues without an interpretation because it's going from earth to heaven and we're speaking mysteries to God (2 Cor. 14:2). When it's a message from God to earth, there should always be an interpretation, either from the one speaking in tongues or another person present.

For Every Believer

How do we know this is for everyone and not just for a special few? Acts 10:34: "Then Peter opened his mouth and said, Of a truth I perceive that God is no respecter of persons." And Acts 2:38 and 39: "Then Peter said unto them, Repent and be baptized (whelmed into the body of Christ) every one of you in the Name of Jesus Christ for the remission of sins, and ye shall receive the gift of the Holy Ghost. For the promise is unto you and to your children, and to <u>all</u> that are afar off (in the future), even as many as the Lord our God shall call."

If you accepted Jesus as your Saviour, you were called and you answered the call, so this promise of the Baptism of the Holy Spirit is for you.

For You Now

We're shown God's desire for this gift for each believer in Luke 11:11-13: "If a son shall ask bread of any of you that is a father, will he give him a stone? Or if he ask a fish will he for a fish give him a serpent? Or if he shall ask an egg, will he offer him a scorpion? If ye then being evil, know how to give good gifts unto your children: how much more shall your heavenly Father give the Holy Spirit to them that ask Him?"

Realize that the language will come from your innermost being not from your head or carnal mind -- just as laughter and crying come from your inner being. You don't think, "Boo hoo or ha, ha, ho, ho." The sounds come up spontaneously, and so will your language as you speak out in faith. It's up to you to speak, to make the sounds. No where in the Bible does it say the Holy Spirit prays or speaks in tongues. We do the speaking. As you make the sound, the Holy Spirit will take over and form the sounds into your own unique tongue. All He needs is our cooperation, our vocal chords, our lips and tongue, for us to yield and make the utterance.

Be expectant! Pray: "Thank you for saving me! Thank you that I have eternal life. I want to serve you with my whole heart, but I need your power. I need more of you! And right now I open my heart even more to receive more of you. Baptize me with Your Holy Spirit! Fill me with your Holy Spirit! I want to praise you in tongues." Allow the sounds to bubble up from inside and in faith speak out the sounds, and Holy Spirit will give you your own special language.

Now the devil will try to steal this away from you. He'll put thoughts into your head like, "That was just an emotional experience. Or that's just gibberish. Or you received the other day, but now you've just memorized those sounds and you're not really praying in tongues anymore. Or, look what you did ten minutes ago. You don't deserve to pray in tongues." That's right. None of us deserve to pray in tongues. So tell the devil, "That's right I don't deserve to pray in tongues. I *need* to." And scold the devil by rebuking him in tongues.

Receiving is just the beginning. It's the doorway to a deeper spiritual dimension. Continue praying in tongues throughout your day every day, and you'll see a difference in your life.

Epilogue

I received this email from Paul who calls me his spiritual mom, and it made me cry in thanksgiving and gratefulness to God for what He has done. Paul is a five-fold ministry Teacher and receives the most amazing revelations from God.

June 10, 2010

Honey,

> Mainly you and Kenneth Copeland played the most impact in my life. Kenneth taught about faith but you showed me about faith. Kenneth taught me about Love but you showed me Love. Kenneth taught about the Gifts but you showed me the Gifts. Ken taught to pray in the Spirit and you showed how to and that it's all right to use it all the time.

> I look back and see how special CMC was. It's funny to say prison is a good thing, but God had all the right people in place there. I can recall how scared I was to talk to you, but I was so hungry for God and so carnal. I hope and pray

that God has filled the gap in CMC.

Thank you for teaching me how to be a Christian on the Job and in the face of Danger. You were so tiny and there was so much evil in that place. Your Love for Jesus always is in the fore front of my mind. It testifies to me anytime someone does not agree with the Spirit or The Gifts or the Boldness and Love, to obey Jesus, to Stand and Walk alone no matter what.

Love,

Your spiritual son, Paul

Paul,

I know sometimes I was really scared going into some of the assignments! Not scared of inmates so much as scared I didn't know the duties and would look inept as an officer...like dining rooms. But God took care of me and increased my faith thru my obeying and doing Vacation Relief when I was scared to death of it!

But sometimes I'd be so sad about a difficult situation, and you were really an encourager and helped so much!!!

And I remember when God told you not to read the three books written by men of God that you wanted to read so much. I knew you were struggling and explained what a privilege it was that God wanted to teach you HIMSELF. And praise God you gave the books away before reading them. And look at you NOW!

And I remember we were standing on a porch during chow release and you were explaining a fresh revelation God gave you soon after you gave those books away, and I was in awe and realized then for the first time how God will use you mightily in the future.

And I remember when you, David, and I were at the cafeteria in Los Angeles, and the teaching anointing fell on you. I had tears in my eyes because of the greatness of God and how I had hoped the three of us could get together one day, and it happened! The three of us were together again, praying and praising the Lord together!

Love,

Your spiritual mom, Honey

And what a thrill and a joy it is to see how an officer I've mentored over the years, Shawn Hardin, is being used to transform staff, inmates, and the atmosphere wherever God sends her at her prison.

Once, God had her tell staff, "God says there's going to be a riot soon. But it's going to happen while I'm gone."

As tensions heightened, she said, "Relax. I told you the riot is going to happen when I'm not here."

And sure enough, there was a riot on her days off.

And a captain asked her awhile ago, "Is God telling you anything lately?"

Yes, staff learned that God gives His children wisdom!

And God even brought my husband and me together in a supernatural way. But then, that's another story of Jesus' love and grace -- !

My next book will relate how God brought my prophet husband and me together supernaturally through dreams, visions, and Word of Knowledge. It will also include others' God-arranged romances. God is concerned about who we marry! And He has a tender, romantic heart! And now that I'm widowed, I'm wondering how He'll have me meet my next and last husband.

Wayward Years

Current

Spiritual sons, Paul and David

Current

About the Author

Honey is widowed and shares heart to heart about her traumatic childhood and years of suffering physical, emotional, and verbal abuse. God uses her transparency to encourage, inspire and heal the wounded heart through the gifts of the Spirit and teaches on how to stand for God's promises until fulfillment.

Honey wrote monthly articles in A Word from the Rib Magazine for several years, has had several hour-long TV interviews, and has ministered at Aglow and church retreats in Arizona and Missouri -- and in churches in Bangkok, Taipei, Mexico, the Philippines, Florida, N. Carolina, and throughout California.

In the Philippines and Peru, she preached at crusades, a youth conference, churches, and taught pastors at a bible college there in Cebu. When she is in Arizona, the Chaplain has her minister in six services. She now conducts CA State prison chapel services twice a month.

She has had the joy of seeing God save, deliver, and heal

people emotionally and physically from blindness, ruptured discs, migraine headaches, crippled knees, arthritis, etc. God has baptized hundreds in the Holy Spirit from little children to tough bikers and people who have sought the baptism for over 30 years. God arranges for this to happen wherever she goes: to window cleaners and servers in restaurants and strangers in trains, planes, airports, department stores, and over the phone.

She became one of the first women correctional officers in a prison housing male felons. Jesus baptized her in the Holy Spirit while she was alone in a gun tower after midnight. She had the joy of watching God transform hardened inmates and staff and her rebellious son, and also save her daughter and her parents and heal their turbulent marriage.

In answer to specific prayer, God showed her who her second husband was to be through dreams, visions, and Word of Knowledge. Twenty-one years later, Honey found God's grace is sufficient for all things during her husband's illness and death. She felt His love, peace, comfort, and enabling strength supporting her in a very tangible way. Jesus is everything to her!

Honey is licensed as an evangelist under Capstone International Ministry and is available for speaking engagements and retreats.

Honey is available for speaking engagements and retreats.

www.HoneyFromTheRockMinistry.com
P. O. Box 775
Grover Beach, California 93483